W9-BEC-251

Only
the
Best

A Celebration of Gift Giving in America

Only the Best

HARRY N. ABRAMS, INC., PUBLISHERS, NEW YORK

TEXT BY JILL SPALDING

INTRODUCTION BY LETITIA BALDRIGE

BY *Stuart E. Jacobson*

PHOTOGRAPHY BY JESSE GERSTEIN

DESIGN BY JOHN LYNCH

The overleaf depicts the
living room in the New York apartment
of Mr. and Mrs. R. Thornton Wilson.
The eighteenth-century boiserie and parquet floors
are from Versailles and were a wedding gift
to R. Thornton Wilson's father and mother
from his aunts, Mrs. Cornelius Vanderbilt
and Mrs. Robert Goelet.

ONLY THE BEST: A Celebration of Gift Giving in America is a
production of Redtree Associates, Inc., Washington, D.C., in
association with Jane Lahr in New York.

Project Manager: Alvin Rosenbaum
Editors: Maura Kennedy and Ruth Eisenstein

First printing 1985

Library of Congress Cataloguing in Publication Data

Jacobson, Stuart E.
  Only the best.

  1. Gifts—United States. 2. Gifts—United States—
History. 3. Celebrities—United States. I. Spalding,
Jill. II. Gerstein, Jesse. III. Title.
GT3041.U6J33   1985   394   85-7327
ISBN 0-8109-1483-2

Printed and bound in Japan.

*G*iving is what this book is all about, and it is dedicated to the seven people whose gifts of enthusiasm, excitement, and belief were crucial to the completion of a project that has proved to be the most exhilarating experience of my life: Ruth and Coleman Jacobson, my mother and father, who stood behind me the entire way; Lupe Murchison, who urged me on in more ways than I can count; Walter Annenberg, whose shared reminiscences sparked the idea underlying the book; Stanley Marcus, whose standards of the highest quality have been a continual inspiration; Roger Horchow, who has been a guide and mentor *and* introduced me to Letitia Baldrige; and Mildred Knopf, my oldest and youngest friend, who not only supplied moral support when I needed it, but also introduced me to many of the people whose stories are in this book.

ACKNOWLEDGMENTS

Special thanks are due to a number of people whose support of this project, and faith in it, played a major part in making it a reality. I gratefully acknowledge the assistance of William and Mary Elizabeth Boren, Delphae Boyd, J. Baxter Brinkmann, Carol Rae Brock, Charlsie Burden, Mrs. Effie Cain, Michael J. and Wynelle Collins, Douglas and Mary Covington, Anthony C. de Bruyn, Brooke Stollenwerck Frampton, Linda V. Gray, Leslie Sinclair Holman, Sally Sharp Jacobson, Mrs. Belton Kleberg Johnson, Kathlene D. King, Catherine E. Kruse, Bruce E. Lazarus, Patricia Patterson Lebermann, Judith Abrams Lifson, Richard H. Luders, Jane T. O'Toole, James R. and Allison Browning Poage, Leon and Idelle Rabin, Marilyn Rolnick, Carolyn T. Shamis, Diana Strauss, Frederic F. Wiedemann, Trisha Wilson, Lois C. Wolf, A. Wayne Wright. I am indebted as well to all those who told me their stories and treated me as a friend.

I wish to express my appreciation also to the many others who have helped at various times and in various ways: Cathy Abshire, Tice Alexander, Rupert Allan, Lynn Almada, Lee Anderson, Earl Angstedt, Bill Arndt, Jerry Arterburn, Sandy Avchen, Edward Balut, Louis Barnes, Clay M. Basham, Norman and Harriet Beck, Vera Benlian, A. Scott Berg, Marsha Berger, Fred Bernstein, Sue Blair, Linda Blanton, Barbara Boehm, Nicholas Bongard, Katharine Boychuck, Joyce Boyum, Pamela Hope Brack, Vol Brashears, Victor Brasso, Nancy Brinker, Constance Brooks, Linda Brooks, Jeff Burkhart, Jerry H. Buss, Bill Butler, Eric Butler, Kelly Campbell, Allan Carr, Jean Carr, Edward Lee Cave, Debbie Cherney, Lauren Childress, Derrell Childs, George Christy, Linda Cohen, Barbara Jeanne Coffman, Betty Cooper, Lorna Corbett, Cliff Counts, Jean Crehan, Brando Crespi, Count Rudolph Crespi, Elaine Crispin, John Cronin, Joel Curtis, Fredericka Davis, Gates Davison, Kim Dawson, Dennis Decker, Nancy Dickerson, Andrea Disocebran, June M. Douglas, Sharman Douglas, Kathy Ellingsworth, Ray Eng, Franz Etienne, Linda Faulkner, Irving Fein, Ron Ferg, Thomas Fetzek, Laurie Firestone, Shirlee Fonda, Joan Fontaine, Christopher Forbes, Jim Frasher, Bill Frye, Sue Gallo, Duanne Garrison, Kathy Gerrie, Fred Gibbons, Myles Goertz, Arthur Gold, Wendy Goldberg, Milton Goldman, John and Louise Good, Kenn Gray, Ellen Green, Judy Green, Gary Grether, Ayn Grinstein, Leonard and Jane Haber, Tom Hahn, Ray Hailey, Ashton Hawkins, Marvin Heifferman, Mac Hoak, Elizabeth Hogan, Jay Hollenberger, Nancy Holmes, Thomas and Nancy Hoving, Fred Hughes, Lenita Hughes, Christoper Idone, Leon Irwin III, Susan Jacobson, Earl James, Betsy Jentz, Marvin and Eliza Johnson, Sara Johnson, Pete Jones, Ray Jones, Stan Kamen, Rick Kammerer, June Keenan, Margret Kelly, Jackie Kendall, Nabila Khashoggi, Eugene Kilgore, Chad Kirkham, Perry Knowlton, Harry Kraut, Sonia Kundert, Steve Kuzcko, Jack Langdon, Roger LeClaire, Leo Lehrman, Cleva Lichtenwald, Dee Lily, Freddi Lindsey, John Littlejohn, John Loring, Brenda Lubojasky, Kendall Lutkins, Cyril Magnin, Laura Mako, Candace Marcum, Diana Markes, Daniel Martin, Jerry Martin, Gregg Marx, Frank McCarthy, Mitchell McLean, Dean Meadors, Sarah Melvin, Joan Miller, Luta Miller, Virginia Milner, Toni Mindling, Holly Russell Moore, Penelope Moorehead, Francis Mossiker, Jane Mulkey, Keith Nix, Katharine Norris, Joe Norton, Michael O'Connor, Jack O'Shea, David Ober, Laurel Overman, Murry E. Page, Monique Pannagio, Betsy Parish, Bob Parish, David Payne, Carolyn Peachy, Becky Pearson, Kathy Petronis, Irene Phelps, Vine Phoenix, Barbara Poe, Vicki Pribble, Dallas Prince, Gloria Ravitch, Robert Reck, John Redford, Nancy Reed, Pascal Regan, Tally Richards, Kathryn Ritchie, Susan Roach, Ralph Rogers, Kyle D. Romans, Susan Porter Rose, Kurt Ross, Phyllis Rowan, Barbara Russell, Chen Sam, Mikal Sandoval, Jim Sanford, Mary Sanford, Mozelle Sauls, Patricia Schmidt, Ramona Scholder, Mark Segal, John Sibley, Stanley Silberstein, Patricia Sinnott, Milton Sladen, Robert Slatzer, Arthur Slaughter, Nena Smith, Alice Snavely, Michael Snead, Juana Snyder, Jack Soden, Stuart Soloway, Randy Spence, Lynn Sponseller, Jewel Staffelbach, Virginia Stanton, Wendy Stark, Jack Starr, Margret Stearns, Bob Steiner, Kate Stern, Jane Stewart, Burl Stiff, Connie Stone, Nancy Strauss, Nan Summerfield, Michael Teague, John M. Theirl, Jo Throckmorton, Betty Tilson, Bobbie To, Mary Tydings, Rudy Vallee, Maryellen Vandivier, Connie Wald, David Walker, John White, Irene Wiley, Hutton Wilkinson, Jeanne Willsey, Christina Wyeth, and Chloe Zerwick.   *S.E.J.*

Contents

INTRODUCTION

*R*oger Horchow of the catalogue world called me one day from Dallas and asked me to see in my New York office a young friend of his, Stuart Edward Jacobson, a fellow Texan whom Roger had time only to describe as "a man with an idea."

When Mr. Jacobson called for an appointment, I apologized in advance for the fact that our meeting would be very short—ten minutes at the outside. He walked into my office with an infectious grin, which I later discovered rarely leaves his face—a handsome blond young man meticulously dressed in a well-fitting gray flannel suit, the perfect shirt and tie, and well-polished shoes. I decided I liked him if for nothing more than his ready smile and well-groomed appearance.

He then proceeded to hold my attention for well over an hour on the subject of his "idea" with a degree of enthusiasm that put me in mind of a concert pianist swelling to a great crescendo, or a runaway express gathering speed! By the time he had finished, I was ready to go find him backers, or publish the book myself on borrowed funds, or do anything to help him reach his goal—a rather simple one at that. He just wanted to produce the best book on the subject of great gifts that had ever been published. It happens to be a subject that has

long fascinated me, too, even before the Kennedy days in the White House, when I was in charge of the state gifts that were given by our President and First Lady.

Stuart in fact did not need my help. He had an ample supply of energy, adrenaline, or whatever other natural source is required to enable one to tackle the impossible and make it happen. He began his research and in a matter of weeks he was ticking off one by one the names of prominent people. They found it hard to say no to him; the rich and the famous divulged their best gift stories, some with nostalgic reticence, others with unrestrained relish.

With traveling iron, shoe polish, and a plethora of clean shirts in his suitcase, Stuart traveled the country for a year, interviewing celebrities. He persuaded *Vogue*'s Jill Spalding to undertake the writing, then corralled Jesse Gerstein to record in color the unusual gifts that pepper these pages.

This author had not exactly led a humdrum life before becoming "Monsieur le Cadeau," as he was affectionately dubbed by some French friends. The idea for this project came when he was sitting with his father in the living room of President Reagan's great friend Walter Annenberg in the latter's Palm Springs home. He listened to Annenberg's reminiscences of the night in 1949 when Winston Churchill gave him an autographed picture after a conversation during a stag dinner hosted by Bernard Baruch, and how much this gift had meant to him over the years. Stuart then listened to the general discussion on the wedding gifts that were being dispatched to Prince Charles and Princess Diana, and he thought about his family's friendship with Stanley Marcus, the acknowledged dean of gift givers.

The science and the art of gift giving have come together in this book. The pages are dramatized by wonderful photographs and anecdotes laced with history, sentiment, materialism, the art of timing, and the urges of love, humor, and revenge—in short, everything connected with the emotions of giving and receiving. The book is great fun to read. It's a wander through the history of gift gossip as well as a sociological reflection of the changing society of America. The reader may be aghast at the profligacy in some of the stories, be touched by the imagination and subtlety of some of the gifts, and at other times be stunned by the magnificence of the houses and jewels presented with the insouciance of someone passing around a box of chocolates.

Each reader will find his or her favorite stories of gifts in these pages. I certainly have mine, particularly those involving patience and love—not just money. I wept, for example, reading about the late Henry Fonda's gift to Katharine Hepburn not long before the end of his life. . . . I was filled with admiration, not only for the donor's incredible craftsmanship but also for the recipient who had inspired such love, when I read about Mildred Knopf's gift to Angela Lansbury. . . . I laughed at Art Buchwald's ingenuity in deciding on the perfect gift for Robert and Ethel Kennedy's seventeenth wedding anniversary. . . . I loved Marietta Tree's imagination in commissioning a painting as a gift for her husband, Ronnie. . . . Over and over, I admired the grace with which good friends thought of each other.

The heart and soul of giving shines through all these pages of celebrity glamour and glitter. History does, too. I, for one, wouldn't have minded being a guest at the late 1800s debut ball of Consuelo Vanderbilt in Newport at the cozy family place, Marble House. The guests all received favors—jeweled and enameled bibelots from the Versailles court of the French kings. Eighteenth-century French things weren't even in vogue at the time of the ball, but the Vanderbilts sensed they were on to something. They had what's called *style*.

You'll find a lot of that in these pages, too.

Letitia Baldrige

PREFACE

Gift giving in America is a tradition and a talent. We give gifts the way we go to the office, routinely and continually—if not always as conventionally. Reflecting our tendency to flamboyance and our inclination for the sentimental, gift giving in America has reached from the gilded edges of the marketplace to the innermost corners of the heart.

In the gift exchange ritual, there are the givers and the receivers, and between them is an intricate pattern of motivation and emotion that makes up the gift relationship. To be a great giver, a great receiver—each is an art. The great giver is a breed apart, sometime angel, sometime fool, at once in and out of control, but always operating from the heart.

America's social history documents its givers with zest and with pride. There was merchant banker August Belmont, who entertained two hundred regularly for dinner, spent twenty thousand dollars a month on wine, gave real estate away in blocks, and returned home to his wife from travels abroad with twelve steamer trunks of tokens for her. There was land baron John Jacob Astor IV, who carried thousands in loose change for "impulse buying"; bon vivant Diamond Jim Brady, who distributed over two million dollars' worth of trinkets in his lifetime, rewarding those of his guests who survived his Lucullan feasts with thousand-dollar diamond-studded favors; William Randolph Hearst, whose only way of giving Marion Davies houses was in multiples; and Marion Davies herself, who once took twenty-six friends to Paris with instructions to buy anything they liked and charge it to her. Closer to our own time, Elvis Presley would hand out Cadillacs by the dozen; Frank Sinatra has orchestrated extravaganzas in Las Vegas so that his pals could enjoy the birthday of a lifetime; and Sammy Davis Jr. has proffered gold cigarette lighters as though they were candy. Mary Martin has stitched needlepoint after needlepoint in painstaking tribute to her friends, holding their value to be "not the pillows themselves but my thoughts as I worked on them." Stanley Marcus, purveyor of the world's most glamorous gifts, found a way to capitalize on a talent that gives him pleasure: there is no task he enjoys more, he once said, than organizing "the treasure hunt, the multiple gifts around a theme which heighten the adrenaline of the recipient."

Equally an art is the talent for receiving. Social history has been less than kind to those gifted ones of legend who ate hearts for breakfast and collected presents like postage stamps. For the most part, what survives of these noted magnets documents their lack of finesse. The capricious Sarah Turnbull, belle of the eighteenth-century South, was said to have received one hundred proposals of marriage; she kept one box filled with colored handkerchiefs and another with jewels, all gifts from her suitors, and delighted in wearing the favors of one hopeful when in the company of another. Mae West, ever guileless, allowed that she "hadn't started out to collect diamonds but somehow they just piled up on me." The high-handed Zelda Fitzgerald in a moment of pique once threw her diamond wristwatch, F. Scott Fitzgerald's first expensive gift to her, out the window of a moving

Above, Richard and Henrietta King.
Right, the La Peregrina pearl.

train. That the biting tongue of Hollywood's formidable columnist Hedda Hopper could be propitiated by treats was evidenced by the legendary lineup of gifts outside her house every Christmas. There was the fecklessness of Isadora Duncan, about whom Diana Vreeland observed, "She was given everything, her living, her food, her champagne, her children." Wallis Simpson's knack of soliciting tangible testimonials from her royal suitor provoked the awe of her contemporaries; "Mrs. Simpson is lucky," confided one to her diary, "and benefits where all others have lost—she has over a hundred thousand pounds' worth of jewels from him!! To say nothing of clothes and furs and things she never had before."

Decidedly, the talented recipient should muster something more ingenuous: a sense of wonder, perhaps, an open delight, a manifest gratitude that strikes just the right balance between discomposure and glee. In order not to flurry her parish, Henrietta King had enameled over with black the diamond earrings her husband, Captain Richard King, bought her with the first profits from what would become the largest privately-owned ranch in America—a move commendable for its delicacy. But surely more gratifying to the donor was the modest suggestion with which Caroline Belmont answered her husband's query as to what to buy her in Paris: "I know you will bring me loads of things, but sometimes cheap *nouveautés* add more to a dress than those expensive items." Marilyn Monroe once fretted for days over how to decline the gift of an elephant from a maharajah, finally pleading that her house was just too small; the enjoyment with which Tallulah Bankhead promenaded her gift leopard around the streets of New York (walking him, to be sure, on a very tight leash) may have been more appropriate.

Finally, the talented recipient has learned to hold every gift in equal value—by which standard Elizabeth Taylor is the greatest receiver of them all. Privately and for the press, America's most beautiful woman craved and wore and reveled in the extravagant sequence of love tokens from Richard Burton, her husband of two marriages: the rare-as-lynx and soft-as-sable kojah fur coat, the fantastic La Peregrina pearl, and the fabled 69.42-carat Taylor-Burton diamond (at $1.05 million, the most expensive single diamond ever sold). But only her assistant will tell you about the painting given to Elizabeth by a blind woman which touched the recipient so deeply that she hung it in her living room in the place of a Renoir.

The history of gift giving in America rainbows from the obligatory to the impulsive, from the profligate to the perfunctory, from munificence to dalliance. Waltzing giddily through ballrooms of sparkling tiaras, it also walks quietly among tables and chairs in the everyday world of Who's for tennis? and What's for dinner? and By the way, darling, I brought you some flowers. At its most conventional, it is the ritual of exchanged merchandise as prescribed by Hallmark cards; at its silliest, it is the fifteen-thousand-dollar collar Tiffany made for Mrs. Howard Gould to give to her dog. At its most self-serving, it is Admiral Farragut's inspiration—so pleased was he with a sword with which the Union Club honored him as the most popular man in the Navy—to have a diminutive copy of it fashioned as a brooch for his wife.

But at its finest, giving in America has been inspired and thoughtful and imaginative and gracious. It is the music box Mark Twain gave to his daughter "because it's Monday." It is the Cadillac artist Billy Al Bengston gave to his colleague De Wain Valentine "because he wanted it."

Giving at its best is not the condition of a close relationship but its symptom, its wrapping and its ribbon, shining and continuous. It is the humor of Carole Lombard's valentine gift to Clark Gable, known for his love of fast cars: a jalopy from the junkyard, which she had painted with red hearts and the message "You're Driving Me Crazy." It is the lavishness of Gable's return gift to Lombard: a ruby ring packaged in a yellow Lincoln convertible. It is the refinement of her gift to him the first year of their marriage: white pajamas and a robe fashioned after her own design out of the last silk to leave China before the Japanese invasion.

Giving at its finest is expressed in the hit song of 1928 "I Can't Give You Anything but Love." Giving at its purest is the spirit of O. Henry's newlyweds; he sold his prized pocket watch so that he could buy her combs for her long silken hair, and she sold her hair so that she could afford a chain for his watch. Giving at its fullest is not a convention, a tradition, or an obligation; it is a state of heart.

NELSON ROCKEFELLER
To
HAPPY ROCKEFELLER

As the grandson of John D. Rockefeller, the Standard Oil king, Nelson Rockefeller was raised to be purposeful, productive, practical, and a dedicated citizen, with little time out for romance and none for extravagance. Whether as patron of the arts, as president of two agencies for economic cooperation, as governor of New York, or, ultimately, as vice president of the United States, Nelson subscribed willingly to his family's stewardship tradition.

But when Nelson married Happy Murphy in 1963, he found happiness of a different sort. It is joyously expressed in this sculpture by Henry Moore, *Rocking Chair No. 1,* which illuminates the tenderness between a mother and her child. Nelson gave it to his wife for Christmas following the birth of one of their sons, and it is Happy's greatest treasure.

THE

Romantic

GIFT

Above, Mary Lily and Henry M. Flagler.

*G*ifts to a loved one are as old as love itself, perhaps going back to the day when Eve first shared with Adam the choicest apple on Eden's tree. Happily, the consequences have not always been so fateful—nor the gifts so perishable. Fruit and flowers have come down to our day as expressions of greeting and affection, rivaled, since its debut in the early 1900s, by countless profferings of the cuddly Teddy Bear. But for the most part history prefers to document the glitter, not the fluff.

In the early days of America, of course, most of what glittered was not gold. There was not much time or energy left over from the deep preoccupation with life and liberty for the pursuit of precious gems in pretty settings. Goods were wrested from the earth. Money was in short supply. Cash transactions of any magnitude were confined to a few wealthy colonists on Beacon Hill.

Then California struck gold, and a decade later, silver. By 1852 New York banks were receiving a hundred thousand gold bars weekly, launching America's new rich on a spending spree that would falter only with the Great Depression. As gold became more abundant, so did visible protestations of love. We read of garnets "strewn on the ground" before the vivacious actress Lola Montez, of sewing-machine heir Paris Singer, who had fathered a son by Isadora Duncan, "besieging her with costly baubles" such as the Cartier diamond necklace she later pawned. Tiffany records sales ranging from two hundred to five thousand dollars' worth of sweet nothings on the order of the jeweled garters and paired hearts that were held acceptable for one's girlfriend of the moment—tangible proof that neither gems nor love was a scarce resource. These were the 1900s, the era of the kept woman, when it was assumed that every gentleman of substance had his "bit of fluff."

Wives did not come any cheaper. William Backhouse Astor outfitted Caroline for her march to the title of *the* Mrs. Astor in a necklace of forty-four remarkably large diamonds, another of 282 marginally smaller ones, and Marie Antoinette's diamond stomacher—worn over an incrustation of gold paillettes with a few spare, if not insignificant, strands flung backward down her spine (which would explain her celebrated posture). Potter Palmer had a fondness for literally covering his wife in diamonds, which may have been relevant to her apotheosis as Chicago's leading hostess.

"There she stands," he would beam, "with half a million on her back."

The Edwardians, who invented taste, drew back from such vulgar displays into the refinement of those ubiquitous rows of pearls that cascade down their bosoms in portraits by Whistler and Sargent. Naturally, the pearls were the size of plovers' eggs, flawless and matched to the millimeter, and valued at a million. In the deal of the decade, Cartier acquired its headquarters by trading just such a strand with Mrs. Morgan Plant for her mansion on Fifth Avenue—a transaction that startled even her contemporaries, since the only token of esteem that outclassed a fine jewel was prime real estate.

To bestow a house on one's consort was the ultimate expression of commitment, doubling nicely as a guaranteed rung up the ladder of Society. August Belmont, the lately arrived and newly rich representative of the House of Rothschild, was so delighted to win the hand of dainty, old-family Caroline Perry (the Commodore's daughter), that he presented her, for their engagement, with an entire block of Manhattan. He followed through for their wedding with a residence on Fifth Avenue. It was the first to have its own ballroom and to own rather than rent its gilded chairs and the requisite red carpet that was rolled along the sidewalk the nights they entertained. These niceties accorded them a coveted box at the opera, which Mrs. Belmont unfailingly occupied on the night of her annual ball to show her freedom from domestic anxieties.

So eager was William K. Vanderbilt that his wife, Alva, outrace his sister-in-law, Alice, for the title of *the* Mrs. Vanderbilt, that he commissioned fashionable architect Richard Morris Hunt to build the costliest mansion in New York. Three million dollars later, Alva had to acknowledge that her gabled and turreted fantasy at 660 Fifth Avenue did not outclass the home of her father-in-law, William Henry, at 664 (the contents of which had been valued at one and a half million dollars and took fifteen outsize volumes to catalogue); she promptly lodged a request for a cottage in Newport that would be outshone by none. William K., whose fortune bore a resemblance to the U.S. Treasury, readily supported with eleven million dollars his architect's pledge to deliver the most sumptuous residence in America. Indeed, so resplendent were its finishings, its furnishings, and the profusion of Italian white marble, which extended even to its driveway, that Marble House would have won Alva her coveted crown—had Cornelius II not placed

Alice first at the finish line with The Breakers. Its Corinthian columns, bathrooms piped with fresh and salt water, front door that weighed seventy tons, fence that cost five thousand dollars a year to paint, and furnishings beyond appraisal simply pulverized Newport. By this time, the title no longer interested Alva; she was now Mrs. O.H.P. Belmont and boasted not just one cozy cottage in Newport, but two.

When Newport ran out of ocean front, the big spenders moved to Palm Beach. In 1901, as one of his wedding gifts to his third wife, Henry M. Flagler used two and a half million dollars of his Standard Oil fortune to construct Whitehall, an extravaganza of bronze doors and gold-fitted bathrooms. (He had already bestowed upon her a large personal check and a flawless strand of pearls, which brought the wedding tote up to four million dollars.) The staggering total of seventy-three rooms opened from a forty-thousand-square-foot marble foyer that made Flagler so uncomfortable he used only the side entrance. Years later, he confessed to a friend, "I wish I could swap it for a little shack."

In no time at all, Palm Beach's Ocean Boulevard became the repository of wedding presents. In 1905, Charles M. Schwab, the President of Carnegie Steel, who is remembered as the financier who broke the bank in Monte Carlo, consolidated the sixty-carat diamond ring he picked out at Tiffany for his wife with a four-million-dollar ocean-front mansion boasting seventy-five rooms, including a gymnasium, a private chapel, and a bowling alley on each floor.

Philadelphia financier Edward T. Stotesbury (who would announce at a dinner for his eightieth birthday, "I have achieved my life's ambition—I have just heard that I am worth one hundred million dollars") worked his way painstakingly up J.P. Morgan's ladder from clerk to senior partner, but his first wife did not live to enjoy his fine fortune. Determined to deny his second wife nothing, he gifted Eva on their wedding day with a diamond tiara, two ropes of pearls, and three million dollars. He then commissioned Addison Mizener to build her a palace in Palm Beach that would show Old Philadelphia the thing or two they had missed in the 145 rooms and fourteen elevators of the Stotesburys' winter residence. In 1920, on the first anniversary of their wedding (which Eva Stotesbury would openly refer to as "the most profitable transaction I have ever completed"), they moved into El Mirasol, described by a former ambassador to

Spain as "far surpassing anything in that country, with the exception only of the Royal Castle." From this suitable setting, Eva orchestrated such stellar events as Mr. Stotesbury's annual birthday party, designed to eclipse the Washington Ball as the social event of the season. Here she reached her apotheosis as *grande dame* of Palm Beach with the extravaganza of her daughter's Valentine's Day wedding to General Douglas MacArthur.

These palaces on Fifth Avenue, in Newport, and in Palm Beach were so transparently bids for social entrée that one has to look elsewhere for the bid for the heart. It was to dazzle his wife, not society, that the eccentric John Ringling, one of the circus brothers, imposed on the stately shores of Sarasota a thirty-room replica of the Palace of the Doges in Venice. It was to express his devotion to Mary Pickford that Douglas Fairbanks had a hunting lodge on fifty-six acres converted into an English manor with sweeping lawns and vistas, which so symbolized the sublime union between Hollywood's sweetheart and its dashing screen idol that the press dubbed it Pickfair and reported on its glittering entertainments long after the marriage itself had tarnished. It was to celebrate their eighth wedding anniversary that Mexican industrialist Bruno Pagliai built for Merle Oberon a villa on the Acapulco coastline and named it Ghalal, which means love. It was to compensate, perhaps, the love of his late life for the divorce he never obtained that publishing king William Randolph Hearst enshrined Marion Davies in accumulating splendor: a townhouse he rebuilt in white marble and costly paneling to reinforce her image as a star; the celebrated castle of San Simeon, in which Marion rattled between the armor and the ketchup bottles, gamely hosting weekends of a hundred guests, half of whom she didn't know; a lavish suite on the twentieth floor of the Ritz Towers, Hearst's Manhattan headquarters. Possibly it was fear that his butterfly might die in all her gilded cages that prompted Hearst's most sensitive gift to her: a Georgian mansion on the sands of Santa Monica. Although it had seventy rooms, a marble swimming pool, ten guest suites, and a cabaret, and though her own bedroom was so long it required a bathroom at either end, Marion's three-million-dollar Beach House was her playground, where she could give her costume parties and escape at whim to ride the roller coaster on the neighboring pier.

"I made the mistake of telling my wife she could have the house she wanted," was the explanation given by tycoon D.J. "Tex" Witherspoon of Omaha for embarking in 1969 on the three-million-dollar construction of a fifty-two-room extravaganza with such household necessities as two swimming pools, a bowling alley, and alcoves for a surfeit of bibelots. But when he learned that his wife was terminally ill, Mr. Witherspoon had crews work around the clock to complete it—which they did just two weeks before she died.

Possibly the most persistent in architectural bids for a fair wife's heart was J. Seward Johnson, the pharmaceutical heir. He built a copy of an English castle for his first wife and an elegant farmhouse for his second. For Barbara, his third wife, forty years his junior, Johnson spared no expense, erecting in Princeton, New Jersey, a twenty-one-million-dollar mansion that took over four years to complete. A hand-cut stone wall a mile and a half long surrounds Jasna Polana. The house itself is built of hand-cut stone and bronze, and its forty rooms with heated marble floors, its indoor tennis courts, its orchid house, its art, and its furnishings are reportedly worth sixty million dollars.

But it is doubtful that any have matched the fervor of Charles Steen, reputedly the only man ever to find uranium in Nevada. In those hopeless years when he was still prospecting, living in a trailer in the desert, he would say to his wife as she washed her nylons in the sand, "When I strike it rich, I'll build you the best house in the world." It was a promise he kept, to the last of twelve million 1950 dollars, persisting in adding such essentials as a moat. The house became known throughout Nevada as Steen's Folly after bad investments had reduced the Steens to eating beans out of cans in the ballroom.

When they ran out of mansions, the great givers turned to gilded transportation. By 1880 the private railway car had emerged as the preeminent hallmark of a traveler's status; every sophisticate had to have one. Jay Gould owned five. "A private car," said Mrs. Belmont, "is not an acquired taste; one takes to it at once."

The first models were a bargain. In the 1870s, Mrs. Leland Stanford paid twenty-five thousand dollars for the car she named for her husband and gave to him on his birthday. By 1920 the cost had escalated to three hundred thousand dollars, and for those glamorized hotel cars whose silken walls and gilded mirrors were destined for more uses than travel, the sky was the limit. The most notorious of these mobile boudoirs was the refulgent

Lalee, originally bestowed on Lillie Langtry, the theater's dazzling beauty, by Manhattan playboy Freddy Gebhard. It went on to greater splendor when Florenz Ziegfeld, maestro of the chorus line, bought it for the pleasure of his young wife, Anna Held, whom he had imported from the music halls of Paris to bask in the limelight of his lavish spectacles and her luxurious milkbaths. Ziegfeld enhanced his initial two-hundred-thousand-dollar investment with a powder room, an observation saloon, a compartment for Anna's tiger cub, a richly upholstered mahogany parlor appointed with stained-glass windows, a piano, and potted ferns. The final flourish was a rear platform designed as a piazza, where, to the music of her five-piece orchestra, Anna could enjoy the scenery—an altogether richer tribute even than the solid-gold statue cast of her by W.H. Millins for the Paris Exposition of 1900.

By now the yacht had metamorphosed from the modest steam paddler of Commodore Vanderbilt's youth through the chandeliered *North Star* of his prime, to Pierpont Morgan's series of increasingly splendid *Corsair*s. Colonel Ned Green had his *United States* cut in half to add a chunk in the middle; this dinosaur of a yacht required two captains, presumably one for each end.

But none approached the glory of the famous *Hussar*. Legend has it that to inspire his new wife with his passion for sailing, and to enhance the six months they often spent on the high seas, E.F. Hutton gave the vessel to Marjorie Merriweather Post. (After they were divorced, she kept the boat, renaming it *Sea Cloud*.) A crew of seventy-two manned this floating palace, the largest sailing yacht ever built, of which it was said, "Even the lifeboats have lifeboats." Guests dined off Sèvres, bathed in marble tubs, and slept in canopied beds.

When bicycling became a novelty, Diamond Jim Brady took to working off his gargantuan dinners (he was known to ingest at one sitting several fowl, up to six lobsters, six dozen oysters, a soufflé made with a dozen eggs, and an entire box of chocolates) on spins around Central Park with his lady love. He commissioned Tiffany to prepare a brace of silver bicycles. Finding the result somewhat sober, he asked that the one destined for Lillian Russell be gold-plated and encrusted with diamonds, but Tiffany declined (somewhat unexpectedly, since they had happily fashioned Diamond Jim's most imaginative gift to Miss Russell, a solid-gold chamberpot embossed at its bottom with an eye). He

Above, Pickfair.

E.F. Hutton
To
Marjorie Merriweather Post

Above, the Hussar *(now called the* Sea Cloud*).*

took his business elsewhere, and for many a Sunday Lillian Russell, presumably Central Park's first flasher, dazzled the birds on her diamond-studded machine. Lillian's taste in gifts was also on the flamboyant side. She presented Diamond Jim with a platinum pocket watch encircled with emeralds.

The introduction of the horseless carriage inaugurated a custom of car giving that continues today, though perhaps not quite with the éclat of the Rolls-Royce that steel magnate James Corrigan presented to his young wife, Laura, on their wedding day, complete with a liveried footman and a chauffeur who, he informed her, came from the estate of Jay Gould.

Although Neiman-Marcus documents a sale in 1960 of a $140,000 His and Her airplane, the allocation of jets to tax-deductible purposes has precluded gestures involving Boeing 707s. One still hears, however, of the occasional Lear jet, like the *Barefoot Baroness* that Ricky Portanova bestowed on his wife, Sandra, to facilitate her hops between Houston, Acapulco, and Europe. Possibly the plushest winged valentine was the *Flying Ginny*, a DC-3 that Texan oil magnate Clint Murchison converted for his wife into a glamorous home-above-home with pastel carpets and etched-glass panels.

Diamonds and palaces, Pullmans and yachts—these were staggering gifts, great public expressions of commitment and devotion, in an age when few worried about conspicuous consumption and none about taxes. Modern times have brought with them a retrenchment of spending but also an expansion of intimacy between people in love. With the new leisure comes the time to search out the unusual and to craft the unique.

We have come full circle, into a contemporary realization that all that glitters need not be gold, that the most meaningful things come in the smallest packages—often in no packages at all. Light-years of feeling separate the sixteen-carat sapphire Reginald Vanderbilt selected for his engagement to Gloria Morgan (a transaction that took exactly twelve minutes) from the ring in a matchbox, "the small, ordinary kind kept in the kitchen," with which catalogue king Roger Horchow first proposed to his wife, Carolyn. "I suggested to her that I was trying to light another kind of fire, and I asked her to open the box, which she did. There, glinting like a tiny sunbeam, was the best engagement ring I could afford at the time."

The romantic gift is personal, like the medallion Dwight Eisenhower commissioned Tiffany to design for Mamie on their fortieth anniversary. Inherently practical, Ike, when he stopped by to settle the bill, jokingly inquired whether his position as President entitled him to a discount. Tiffany's president looked up at the famous portrait of Mary Todd Lincoln wearing the Tiffany pearls her husband had selected for her while he occupied the Oval Office. "Well," he replied, "we didn't give any discount to Mr. Lincoln."

The romantic gift is a messenger, bearing its love in an inscription. When Humphrey Bogart finished *To Have and Have Not*, the film in which he met and fell in love with Lauren Bacall, he sent her a gold I.D. bracelet inscribed "Whistle," in meaningful reference to the film's classic line, "If you want me just whistle."

Bogart's technique was not lost on his director, Howard Hawks For their first wedding anniversary, Hawks took his wife, Dee, to Cairo, where he presented her with a massive gold bracelet made up of eight segments, each embossed with a high point of their first year. On the last segment, tiny rubies spelled out Dee's name—in hieroglyphs.

Bandleader Harry James chose a more literal way to stay close to his wife, Betty Grable, of the glorious legs, who was America's number one pinup girl. He orchestrated a charm bracelet for her out of gold, platinum, and diamonds that depicted himself and the five members of his band.

At its most daring, the object itself spelled out the message, like the slave bracelet Natacha gave to husband Rudolph Valentino. He wore it frequently, despite exhortations of the press to discontinue sporting such an "effeminate article" lest it launch a trend. There was also the notorious exchange between Ann Sheridan, Hollywood's "Oomph girl," and her lover, as reported by jeweler Paul Flato. Flato crafted for him a pair of fly buttons, an emerald and a ruby, signaling "stop" and "go." For her, there was an ankle bracelet on which was spelled out in diamonds, "Heaven's Above."

Though the history of the romantic gift winds its way among pleasures and palaces, diamonds and Daimlers, its essence is immaterial. "Love," says Oscar Hammerstein's lyric in *The Sound of Music*, "isn't love until you give it away."

The romantic gift spans the range of human emotion; it projects into visible form the feelings behind it. Edith Bolling Wilson, in order to ease her husband's transition from an active two-term presidency into retirement, had a grandfather clock made, copying to the last detail of his beloved West-

LILLIAN RUSSELL
To
DIAMOND JIM BRADY

Above, Diamond Jim's watch.

Above, the Flying Ginny.

Above, Betty Grable's bracelet.
Harry James and Betty Grable.

minster chimes Wilson's favorite object in the White House. Helen Gould Shepherd commissioned an Aeolian pipe organ for her husband so that he would feel more at home in Lyndhurst, the five-hundred-acre estate she inherited from her father, Jay Gould. So closely had she met his need that their son wrote in later years of the joy that his father, now blind, experienced playing the organ through the long afternoons.

The romantic gift is no slave to time. Mary Munn of Palm Beach pledged as a wedding gift to her husband, the Earl of Bessborough, a petit point for an heirloom sofa. It took her twenty years to complete the intricate pattern of flowers and birds intertwined in the family crest. She then put it on the train to the local upholsterer—and it was stolen. The next day she began all over again.

The romantic gift embodies a commitment to finding exactly the right thing. According to their contemporaries, there was not a couple better suited in tastes and temperaments than Cole Porter and his wife, Linda Lee. They traveled with both a valet and a lady's maid. (It was said that the latter dressed Linda from hat to stockings and that if no one was around to offer her a light, her cigarette remained unlit.) They devoted as much energy to each other's whims as to their own, exchanging presents that were romantic or frivolous or lavish, but always in great taste. Only occasionally did they misfire: the custom-made sedan Cole gave her one Christmas morning was enthusiastically received but never used because, as Linda explained, the springs bruised her sables. But for the most part they scored—Cole with such ten-thousand-dollar baubles as a ruby-and-platinum box designed by Verdura and a magnificent diamond-and-platinum bracelet from Cartier, Linda with a tradition of bejeweled cigarette cases that she had Verdura specially execute to mark the opening of each of Cole's shows. But it was Cole's final gift to her that expressed most purely his feelings for his partner of thirty-five years: he spent a hundred thousand dollars for the hybridization of a new rose of the most delicate pink, which he dedicated to her memory as the Linda Porter Rose.

The romantic gift is thoughtful. Knowing that for a man of many homes the greatest gift is convenience, Nancy (Mrs. Zubin) Mehta went to great lengths to provide the New York Philharmonic's much-traveled maestro with the same telephone number for their Manhattan brownstone as they have in Los Angeles. "The number had already been

EDITH BOLLING WILSON
To
WOODROW WILSON

Above, Woodrow Wilson's clock.

LYNDON JOHNSON
To
LADY BIRD JOHNSON

COLE PORTER
To
LINDA LEE PORTER

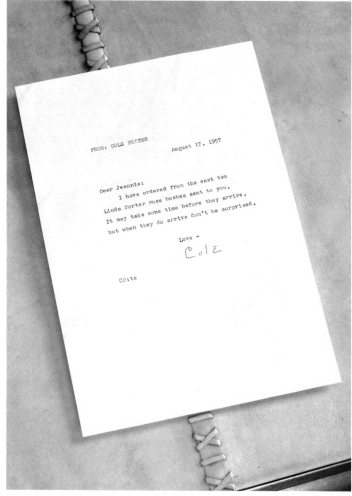

Above, photo Johnson sent to Lady Bird.

Above, Cole Porter's note to Jean Howard.

taken," she says, "but I worked on it for a year and finally got it. When I gave it to him on our anniversary, he couldn't believe it."

The romantic gift is sentimental. Of all the meaningful presents she received from Lyndon B. Johnson, Lady Bird Johnson most cherishes the photograph of him that she had asked him to send her when he returned to his work in Washington after they had first dated in Austin in 1934.

The romantic gift is caring. Denise Hale, wife of the department store magnate, had just lost a dog that she loved as if it were a child when she came across an eighteenth-century porcelain dog in a Sotheby's catalogue and remarked on how it reminded her of her Baby Hale. Seeking for a way to console his wife, Prentis Hale put in a winning bid for the rare Ta Ching figure and presented it to her. Denise was overcome: "I love Chinese Baby Hale more than I can say. He carries on the spirit of our beloved dog."

The romantic gift is imaginative. Charlotte Mailliard, San Francisco's deputy chief of protocol, was inspired after a camp-out in Montana with her outdoors-loving husband to incorporate the bliss of sleeping under the stars into their California ranch house. It was not the simplest of brainstorms, because their bed was a massive four-poster, but she rounded up everyone she knew with some knowledge of mechanics and together they rigged up a motor that ejected the bed through a sliding wall, leaving the bedposts behind. "So if anyone comes looking for us, there will be four posters, with absolutely no one and no bed in the room, because we'll be sleeping out among the redwoods under the wonderful star-studded sky and waking with the birds and the deer all around us and the sheep coming up close, not knowing what's going on."

Arguably, the most romantic gift is that given of oneself. It is certain that the little word poems crafted by e.e. cummings for his adored Marion influenced her decision to become his third wife. It is possible that Irving Berlin, born Israel Baline and raised on the Lower East Side, would not have won the hand of pretty Ellin Mackay, heiress to the great Comstock fortune, if he had not written his best three ballads for her during their courtship. Sculptor Robert Graham tags the ladies in his life with miniature gold figures he fashions into pendants for them, and painter Chuck Arnoldi devised his now-famous twig valentine, with a close semblance of his heart nesting in its center, to persuade Katie to become his wife.

CHARLOTTE MAILLIARD *To* JACK MAILLIARD

Above, the Mailliards' bed.

VERONIQUE PECK
To
GREGORY PECK

Gregory Peck: "In 1966, when we had been married for ten years, Veronique surprised me with the first of a series of anniversary presents (to be given every fifth year, although I did not know that at the time). The first was a Picasso color lithograph, *The Woman with Green Hair*. I had admired it for years, especially since the lady, except for the green hair, could be Veronique.

"On our fifteenth anniversary, a noble bronze horse appeared. It is seventeenth-century Italian, and again it was a complete surprise. Veronique had started a family tradition.

"My twentieth-anniversary gift turned out to be an abstract kinetic sculpture, *Venus*, by Yaacov Agam. It is of brass, gold-plated. The sculptor encourages people to touch and manipulate his works. This *Venus* is particularly interesting: one can spin the three golden disks representing head, heart and womb in the same direction, or create different rhythms by spinning them in different directions at different speeds.

"The twenty-fifth–anniversary present stunned me. It is a bronze figure by Maillol, *Île de France*. The original, five feet high, stands in the gardens of the Louvre. Ours is one of an edition of only six—forty-one inches high, finished and polished by Maillol himself.

"We both enjoy living with these beautiful objects, but what I truly appreciate is that each gift has been so carefully chosen and then somehow transported into our house in total secrecy.

"I don't know how many husbands today are so agreeably spoiled by their wives in this way, but I can't recommend it too highly."

Above, Veronique and Gregory Peck.

Archibald Roosevelt
To
Selwa Roosevelt

Selwa Roosevelt, the distinguished chief of protocol at the White House: "Every gift from my husband brings me joy—but this necklace has a special meaning for me.

"When I was named chief of protocol, we both knew that this meant a vast change in our normally quiet and well-ordered lives. My husband was very proud of me and wanted to give me something both appropriate for the new job and an expression of his pride and faith in me.

"He asked jewelry designer Barbara Witt of San Francisco to make this necklace. I have long admired Barbara's work and Archie knew that I had always wanted a pearl necklace that wasn't like anyone else's pearl necklace. So this was Barbara's creation and I was thrilled with it.

"Now I find I wear it on official and state occasions more than any other piece of jewelry I own. Every time I wear it, I think of the love and support it symbolizes."

Above, Archibald and Selwa Roosevelt.

Ramona Scholder
To
Fritz Scholder

Fritz Scholder is a painter, originally from the Midwest, who lives in New Mexico, in Arizona, and in New York. Hence, "I have three different realities." He could lay claim to a fourth, a spiritual domicile in the Land of the Pharaohs. Scholder has always been fascinated by Egyptology. Once he visited the Valley of the Kings, "where I literally walked on a carpet of mummies with hundreds of bats flying around; it was like one of my great fantasies lived out."

His wife, Ramona, decided that nothing would please her husband more than a vial of powdered mummy, a cure-all that the Victorians believed to be a source of pure energy if sprinkled to taste on poached eggs.

Given that the theory has long since been discredited, it was some years before Ramona located a vestige of the proverbial nostrum in an old apothecary's in New York. She entombed it in an art deco Lalique perfume bottle with an Egyptian motif and gave it to Fritz with pyramids of affectionate wishes for Christmas in 1978.

Above, Fritz and Ramona Scholder.

STEVE MCQUEEN
To
ALI MACGRAW

When she first caught his eye, actor Steve McQueen sent actress Ali MacGraw a bunch of daisies. The gesture apparently failed to spark her interest, since she threw the flowers into the trash can.

The persistent McQueen decided to send her an even larger bunch of daisies—in fact a huge bunch—delicately arranged in a galvanized trash can much like the one shown here.

The technique must have been effective. MacGraw returned the gesture, and from then on, according to Beverly Hills florist Harry Finley, the daisies flew back and forth between them in a variety of trash cans until, eventually, Steve McQueen and Ali MacGraw were married.

Above, Steve McQueen and Ali MacGraw.

CAROLYN HORCHOW
To
ROGER HORCHOW

Selecting the right gift for the purveyor of right gifts is not the easiest of tasks—especially since a man who masterminds a successful luxury gift catalogue is theoretically a man who has everything. But for his fiftieth birthday, Carolyn Horchow thought of the one thing husband Roger did not have and, she thought, would appreciate—a portrait of their daughters, Regen, Elizabeth, and Sally.

Noted Dallas artist Roger Winter does not usually accept commissions, but he was intrigued with her request—a formal portrait in an informal setting. Roger Horchow's birthday is in July, when Texas weather converts the swimming pool into the most appropriate of settings, and where else would a smart Texas family pose at that time of year?

Attesting to Roger's delight with the painting that resulted, the Horchow daughters have top billing in his substantial art collection.

Above, Roger and Carolyn Horchow.

JOHN HAY WHITNEY
To
BETSEY WHITNEY

For their twenty-fifth anniversary, both Betsey Whitney and her husband Jock, the publisher, philanthropist, and sportsman who distinguished himself in the field of Anglo-American relations, came up with the same gift idea—a jeweled tree fashioned by master miniaturist Fulco di Verdura.

The Whitneys and Verdura were close friends, and Verdura had spent many weekends at the Whitney estate, Greentree. There he had observed the symbol of the estate—a beautifully gnarled old tree covered with ivy.

Betsey's commission was straightforward, an exact reproduction of the signature tree. Jock's was more intricate; he wanted a tree with miniature paintings dangling from its branches, each depicting one of their houses—in Georgia, in Kentucky, on Fishers Island, and in New York City.

Four years and eleven million dollars in the making, Alva Smith Vanderbilt's Marble House in Newport, Rhode Island, still stands as one of the most elaborately planned and executed gifts of all time. Completed in 1892, from its ten-ton bronzed entrance grille to the pink Numidian marble dining room to the gilt walls of the Gold Ballroom, it remains one of the most sumptuous private residences ever built in America.

William K. Vanderbilt plotted with architect Richard Morris Hunt to erect and furnish this gem on the beach as a display case for Alva. Unfortunately, he was to spend only two summers admiring her there before she divorced him to marry their neighbor.

WILLIAM K. VANDERBILT
To
ALVA SMITH VANDERBILT

The
True Story
of My
Coat of Arms

by

Charlie McCarthy

FRANCES BERGEN
To
EDGAR BERGEN

Frances Bergen: "The coat of arms story was my husband's brainchild. Edgar thought Charlie should have his own coat of arms, so he drew one up himself and had it printed on matchbooks and stationery, which was used for special thank-you notes; he thought in keeping with the heraldic coat of arms, the envelopes should be sealed with wax. When I was looking around for a present for Edgar, I thought it would be fun to incorporate the coat of arms, so I took the stationery and the wax seal to a jeweler friend of ours in Beverly Hills, Don Hoffman, and asked whether he could create something. He came up with this design of the coat of arms in sealing wax and cast it in gold for cuff links. I gave them to Edgar for his birthday. He was elated and wore them with everything, even a tuxedo. He just loved them. I could not think of anything more permanent than something cast in gold."

Charlie McCarthy's Account of his Coat of Arms:

People seem to find great joy in making disparaging remarks about my ancestors, or lack of same, referring to me as a sapling or splinter. For such insults my valiant forefathers would have demanded satisfaction on the field of honor.

As an exponent of truth, or a reasonable facsimile thereof, I could no longer ignore these verbal poniards, so I decided to delve into the records of lineage heraldry at the library . . .

In practically no time research revealed that all my Gaelic forebears had distinguished court records . . . but most of the judges were lenient. Their war cry, which I use as my motto, was "E Pluribus Mow 'Em Downus," from the Latin meaning, "My fight is your fight . . . Your fight is your own."

With this as a starter, I then discovered that the oak is an emblem of strength, so I tossed in a few oak leaves. This was to show that my family tree is oakey-dokey . . . though somewhat shady.

Realizing that lions in the royal arms are "passant guardant," I added a lion of my own, which is "laughant," and signifies that I am a descendant of the great knight, Sir Laugh-A-Lot.

You will notice there are two knights with pennons flying from their lances. The pennons show which way the wind is blowing. The ostrich plumes are also useful for weather vanes. If they dripped water, the knight knew it was raining. If they went up in smoke, he had been struck by lightning.

Reluctantly, I had to include a bar-sinister dividing the shield. It seems there was some cross-pollination in my family tree. The slant of the bar-sinister means somebody didn't see the minister.

The slingshot represents the legendary arms of the clan McCarthy, and true to tradition, I am an excellent marksman . . . except in my studies. I hold the envious record of not only scoring five consecutive bulls-eyes on Old Pickle Puss, my teacher, while her back was turned . . . but accomplishing this with three-cushioned shots off the blackboard. You will notice the slingshot is backed by a rampant field of rat tails, emblem of the Royal Order of Rat Sluggers, of which I am the Exalted High Rodent. Among the brotherhood I am affectionately known as "Old Rough-On-Rats." . . . The top hat, monocle and white tie is the traditional attire for the McCarthy and marks us as boulevardiers and bon vivants. In plain words, we get around.

Well, that about does it. There you have the plain unvarnished McCarthy! And although my coat of arms may be a little short in the sleeves, the world will be a better place for knowing the facts of my noble heritage.

MARIETTA TREE
To
RONALD TREE

Marietta Tree's most inspired gifts to her husband, Ronald, were renderings of his favorite things. For Christmas 1948, she commissioned this collage of his pipe and reading glasses, a rose, a favored magazine and letter, his scarf, and photos of their home in Barbados and Ronald's English country house, Ditchley.

Equally cherished by Ronald was a series of paintings Marietta commissioned of Ditchley's various rooms. Tree, an Anglo-American who served in the British Ministry of Information and in Parliament during World War II, often accommodated Winston Churchill at Ditchley on evenings when security forces feared the prime minister's residence would be unsafe. Thanks to Marietta's gift, after moving back to America permanently when the war was over, Tree never felt as if he had entirely abandoned his English country house.

Above, paintings of Ditchley.

MILDRED KNOPF
To
EDWIN KNOPF

Mildred Knopf embarked on this rug as a birthday gift for her husband, Metro Goldwyn Mayer producer Edwin Knopf; it pictures all the special times in their life together. Mildred's commentary: *1.* Engaged to be married April 1926. *2.* Married June 24, 1926, at the Villa Charmettes, Biarritz, France. *3.* Our villa at Rapallo, Italy. The S.S. *Roma* was making trial runs and this fascinated Edwin. *4.* With glamour left behind, we returned to New York and lived under the Third Avenue elevated. The yellow truck belonged to Rheingold, my grandfather's brewery. The angel arriving is Christopher. *5.* Edwin's theatre, the auditorium in Baltimore, Maryland. The play was *Peter Ibbetson,* the dream sequence, his favorite. *6.* In 1928, we had our first glimpse of the San Bernardino mountains, the first orange orchards. The second angel, Wendy, was to arrive two years later. *7.* In 1929, Edwin directed his first Western. I was amused at seeing an extra dressed up as an Indian, sitting on a tree trunk

and reading *Variety.* *8.* In 1932, Edwin made movies in Berlin, Germany. We spent Christmas there. Chris and Wendy were dressed as angels. *9.* At St. Moritz, Switzerland, Wendy and Chris regard the wonders of the Alps, 1933. *10.* We spent the spring at the Villa Soleil in Antibes, France. *11.* In the spring of 1933 we went to Boothbay, Maine. *12.* We returned to California in September of '33, in the middle of the Depression. We were broke and grateful to Mildred and Sam Jaffe, who let us live in their Malibu house all winter. *13.* As luck would have it, in the spring of '34 Edwin received three studio offers at the same time. He accepted the offer that paid the least money but offered the best future. He went to MGM, where he stayed for twenty-six years. The angel arriving is Jonathan. *14.* We had a house at Arrowhead Lake. Chris stopped swimming at the hotel beach because they barred his friend Kenny, a black boy. *15.* We were happy at Newport Beach.

Above, Edwin and Mildred Knopf.

The Reagans' devotion to each other is well known. In her autobiography, Nancy says if she could have asked for more, it would have been the proposal of her dreams, "in which he would take me out on a lake in a canoe, play a ukelele, sing to me, and propose as I was reclining with one hand drifting in the water." In love, as in politics, it is never too late to make dreams come true. "On our twenty-fifth wedding anniversary, he gave me a canoe named *TruLuv* and took me out on the lake at our ranch. He did not have a ukelele, but I said it would be all right if he just hummed! It was a sentimental, sweet thing for him to do, and I loved it."

DOROTHY PRICE
To
HICKMAN PRICE

Hardly had former Undersecretary of Commerce Hickman Price settled his new wife into High Tide, the beautiful house overlooking Bailey's Beach in Newport, which he had taken great care in furnishing, than he suffered a heart attack and was advised to move to a house without stairs.

Even though they had found a lovely apartment in New York, Hickman was disconsolate at parting with High Tide and its furnishings; he was particularly attached to the round yellow parlor he had filled with unusually fine pieces that he had acquired during his travels in France. Eventually it was decided at least to keep these; but sensing that even they didn't quite reconcile her husband to the move, Dorothy Price was inspired to have the round yellow room reproduced in a watercolor by artist David Payne as a permanent record of the room and its contents.

Once in Manhattan, they installed the cherished French pieces against the same yellow background with such overwhelming success that, as *his* present to Dorothy, Hickman Price contacted David Payne and had him record them again—this time as they appeared in the square yellow room of their New York apartment.

What do you give one of the richest men in the world? Looking for a meaningful birthday present for her husband, Gordon, the son of oil billionaire J. Paul Getty (provider of a seven-hundred-million-dollar legacy to the museum that bears his name), Ann Getty thought he would be most pleased by a finely wrought replica of the museum's exterior.

To test the waters, she commissioned from Daniel A.J. Martin, known to the trade as "the Fabergé of architecture," a model of their house in San Francisco. Her husband was delighted with this first *tour de force*.

Now confident that Gordon would be pleased with the result, Ann embarked on her next project, charging Martin with the much more exacting task of reducing to scale the J. Paul Getty Museum (designed after a villa near Herculaneum), with its 128 columns, fifty trees, myriad fountains, and classical statuary.

Above, miniature of the Gettys'
San Francisco home.

"TO A LIVING MADONNA"
FROM A LOVING & DEVOTED HUSBAND
1975

MEL ASH
To
MARY KAY ASH

Mary Kay Ash, better known as Mary Kay to the millions of women who have used and sold her cosmetics, recalls: "We were married on a Thursday. One week later, Mel brought me a lovely gift, which he said was  in celebration of our first anniversary. I said, 'Terrific—you mean you're going to do this every week?' Sure enough, the following week he came home with another gift, and the next week with still another, and so on until he died fourteen years later.

"It was not always an expensive gift, of course. It could be anything from diamonds to peanut brittle, but it was always something I wanted or had mentioned, and it was always professionally wrapped and accompanied by a Hallmark card. How could you ever be mad at a man when you come home every Thursday to find a beautiful something or other that he has spent so much time picking out? Another thing he did which was very unusual—he would say 'I love you' at least six times a day."

Among the special Thursday gifts was this Cybis porcelain.

Above, Mary Kay and Mel Ash.

Joseph Oliphant Lambert, Jr.
To
Evelyn Lambert

It is not surprising that the gift Evelyn Lambert treasures most of all from her husband, the well-remembered landscape architect Joe Lambert, who landscaped virtually all Dallas, is the gardens of a ravishing but run-down sixteenth-century villa near Venice they had fallen in love with and bought. His offer to transform the tumble of weeds into an enchantment of ponds and paths and bridges, as a housewarming gift for her, became a labor of love that took eight years and the efforts of twelve workmen. In 1970, Villa Lambert was finished, its three lakes cleaned, its extensive grounds landscaped in the style of "Capability" Brown, the eighteenth-century Englishman whose naturalistic gardens Joe admired. Joe Lambert died the week they moved in, but the gardens live on, delighting the many friends who stop by on the annual tour Evelyn masterminds to support the preservation of Venice.

Above, Joseph and Evelyn Lambert.

Publisher Malcolm S. Forbes bought this Fabergé Imperial Presentation Cigarette Case as a Christmas present for his wife, Roberta, in 1960. While Roberta continued to smoke, Malcolm became hooked on Fabergé. The collection he has assembled over the past quarter of a century is rivaled only by those of the Soviet Government and the Queen of England and is now on permanent display at FORBES magazine's headquarters.

Roberta's cigarette case joined the display only after it had been lost and found. She had dropped it in the snow one winter when leaving a dinner party, and following the spring thaw it was discovered and returned by their hostess.

The Forbeses treasure this piece despite the observation of a scholar hired to catalogue the collection: "Oh—that is the kind of thing that the Czar gave to the stationmaster on state visits."

Above, Malcolm and Roberta Forbes.

MARSHALL FIELD V To JAMEE FIELD

On the occasion of the fortieth birthday of Marshall Field V, scion of Chicago's first family of retail fame and fortune, his wife felt that he deserved something special. Inspired by his love of Early American antiques, she commissioned from noted artist and craftsman Eugene Kupjack a rendering in miniature of the main drawing room of the Nathaniel Russell house in Charleston, South Carolina. The miniature incorporated in exquisite detail (on a scale of one inch to one foot) not only fourteen outstanding examples of Marshall's Early American antiques but also objects as small as a decanter and as delicate as a Renoir pastel. Her husband was so delighted with the result that for Jamee's next Christmas present he commissioned from Kupjack this informal farm kitchen, reproducing her favorite Colonial pieces: Windsor chairs, a trestle table, a bridal chest, and a collection of Pennsylvania pottery copied from Winterthur in exact detail.

Jamee was completely taken by surprise. Her miniature room sits next to Marshall's in the library of their home.

MARTIN GABEL
To
ARLENE FRANCIS

They had met previously, but it was while acting together in a production of *Danton's Death*, directed by Orson Welles, that leading man Martin Gabel and the young actress who would endear herself to millions of Americans as Arlene Francis fell in love and married.

For their first anniversary, Gabel gave Francis her trademark diamond heart pendant. She has worn it so consistently through thirty-seven years of marriage and all her years on television's *What's My Line?* that the one time she appeared on the show without it (the delicate chain had broken), the CBS switchboard lit up with questions about whether the marriage had dissolved, and fans have even written to ask if it was a hearing aid.

"But it wasn't, of course; it was a heart and it meant 'This is where the heart is.' It has diamonds on both sides, which I think is terribly chic—so if I am ever run over they will know it is me.

"I have never taken it off, though I put it on a long chain when I do plays. Martin and I not only have the heart to prove our love; we have a longer record than any play I know."

Above, Martin Gabel and Arlene Francis.

Lynn Wyatt: "We always have a big family Christmas with packages scattered everywhere for all the children, my parents, and my brother. One Christmas morning, I had distributed all the gifts and I had received gifts, but I had for some reason not received any gift from Oscar and I wondered whether it was stuck under the tree somewhere. I wondered if it was so marvelous that he was giving it as a complete surprise. I didn't want to say anything or appear overly anxious, but I was feeling more and more dejected.

"Everyone had opened their gifts, and we were ready to go in for our big Christmas brunch, so I thought, well, maybe I was a bad girl and wasn't going to get anything from my husband. All of a sudden, Oscar said, 'Well, aren't you going to open your present?' And I said, 'What present?' He pointed way up the tree, which went all the way to the ceiling, to an envelope that was perched there. I couldn't imagine what it could be. I said, 'I can't even reach it.' We had to send for a ladder, and it got to be a big thing, with all the family standing around. I opened up the envelope, and there was the deed to this beautiful house, with a divine love note attached and a p.s. that said, 'and the taxes have been paid.'"

Above, the Wyatt home.

JOHN D. MURCHISON
To
LUPE MURCHISON

"I don't want just to hand her a necklace," thought Texas oil king John Murchison, musing over the piece of jewelry he had selected to give his wife for her thirtieth birthday.

Godiva had just come out with a decorative box of chocolates that was heart-shaped and gold-lined. He nestled the necklace into the gold foil so that it would look like the candy wrappers.

"We were watching a Dallas Cowboys football game at dinner," Lupe recalls, "and there had been no mention of my birthday at all. When dessert came, I was presented with this nice box of chocolates—which threw me for a loop, but I didn't say anything because, after all, it is the thought that counts. Then I opened the box to pass the chocolates around and there, hidden among them, was this beautiful necklace."

Above, Lupe and John Murchison.

Moss Hart, the playwright, director, and producer who thrilled Broadway audiences with such hits as *The Man Who Came to Dinner, You Can't Take It with You,* and *My Fair Lady,* had a yen for precious metal, inclining to gold for the least of his accessories. (Kitty would later say that Moss carried so much gold on him that if he ever fell into a pond he would surely drown.)

In 1946, when they were married, Kitty gave Moss a gold tobacco pouch as a wedding present. She consulted Cartier, and they were delighted to oblige, providing Mr. Hart could come in for two fittings to ensure that the pouch would not cause an unsightly bulge in his back pocket, where he wore it.

Kitty Carlisle Hart recalls that at the first fitting they presented her husband with a wooden block on a red-velvet pillow and asked if he would be so good as to slip the wooden block into his pocket. "Moss asked them to hollow it out slightly more, stopped by for a second fitting, and pronounced the block perfect."

The block was then cast in gold, with Hart's monogram on the outside. Inside was the message: "For My Own Dear Love, Kitty."

Above, Moss Hart and Kitty Carlisle on their wedding day.

"Because the horses don't know that Sunday is a day of rest," Marylou Whitney built her first chapel on the grounds of the Whitneys' Kentucky home. Her husband, "Sonny," along with those who tended the horses and the house, appreciated having a place to worship even when duties kept them on the estate.

When the Whitneys moved into Cady Hill House, on their Saratoga Springs estate, an old stagecoach inn, Marylou looked far and wide for inspiration for another chapel for her husband. At last she found it: an 1810 Dutch house. She had the house copied exactly and made a crusade of her hunt for vintage furnishings and architectural fittings. On Christmas Day in 1982, she presented the chapel to "Sonny" at an interdenominational service held to bless it.

Above left, Marylou and Sonny Whitney.
Above, guest book in the Whitney chapel.

DOUGLAS FAIRBANKS, JR.
To
MARY LEE FAIRBANKS

When you have been happily married for forty-six years, as have been the dashing movie star Douglas Fairbanks, Jr., and his lovely wife, Mary Lee, anniversary presents take on the aura of a walk down memory lane.

Pictured here are three of the most meaningful gifts they have exchanged. As befits a gentleman and a scholar, Douglas Fairbanks has been a man of many addresses: Claridge's, Hyde Park, St. James Street, Grosvenor House, Gloucester Place, Park Lane, Chelsea. However, Mary Lee devised a sure way to find him. She

had Cartier design an eighteen-carat-gold envelope with all his addresses engraved on the front, her return address on the back, and inside, her message: "But at last I reached you, My Love, Mary Lee, 1941."

Four years later, Douglas gave Mary Lee a gold compact designed by jeweler George Headley in the shape of a globe. The rubies represent the places they have visited together, and the diamonds signify the places where Douglas was stationed during the war. The compact opens at South America to reveal

compartments for lipstick, comb, and powder.

"To You My Darling on our glorious 38th Anniversary" is the inscription on the lapis box Douglas designed for his wife. It bears gold plaques engraved from the letterheads of the stationery they had used in each of their former homes. "It was, is, and will be, my love," his message to her continues. He signed off with his token, a bug. Mary Lee's pet name for him, "Bug," turns up in his letters to her throughout the years in the form of bugs in all manner of dress and pose.

RICHARD BURTON
To
ELIZABETH TAYLOR

The Burton-Taylor diamonds were the most visible hallmark of the vivid, tempestuous decade of the Burton-Taylor marriages. By their size and by the style with which they were presented, they acquired their own fame, made their own headlines.

There was the 33.19-carat emerald-cut Krupp Diamond Elizabeth won in a wager after beating Richard by a point at Ping-Pong. There was the record-making 69.42-carat Taylor-Burton diamond.

And there was the diamond bracelet, much like the one shown here. Burton arranged for it to be casually entwined in ten dozen Sterling roses (which are in fact lavender, matching Elizabeth's eyes). The flowers were delivered to the Burtons' suite at the Beverly Hills Hotel at precisely 8:30 a.m., since Burton knew Elizabeth would surely answer the door herself. Surely Elizabeth thought she was still dreaming.

Above, Elizabeth Taylor and Richard Burton.

Judy Lewis
To Loretta Young

It was 1961 when the dashing portrait painter Sir Simon Elwes asked Loretta Young if she would do him the favor of sitting for her portrait. He painted it with the proviso that no one buy it, since he needed portraits in order to show his work. Loretta's daughter, Judy, was fascinated by the undertaking and kept making excuses to drop by. One day, Elwes was finished and gone, without Judy having seen his finished work. It had just been whisked away.

After Elwes had died, a New York gallery sent Loretta a catalogue in which the painting was offered, giving her the right of first refusal. Loretta suggested to her daughter that she might want to stop by to see if it was as good a painting as she had remembered.

Judy was so thrilled to find the portrait again that, although it meant mortgaging her salary for the following two years, she felt her mother had to have it. When she showed up on Christmas Day in 1981 with a very large package, her mother knew instantly what it was and was deeply moved: "I love the portrait because, although the mouth looks very sure, the eyes are full of tears. I was going through a lot at that time and Simon saw that, and I remember saying, 'Simon, don't show that.' His reply was, 'That's what I see and that's what I'm going to paint.' And that's why, twenty years later, Judy felt I had to have it and gave it to me as she did. Judy felt that this portrait 'is the essence of Mama.'"

THE GIFT TO A

Child

The doting father, the adoring mother: both are now prototypes of American indulgence, and yet there are few early records of personal presents to small children. The Puritans had little time for levity or for fantasy, and the Victorians had even less. The bonanza dust settled on the end of the nineteenth century, creating an ambience of chilly magnificence whose marbled corridors provided few warm corners for the young.

It is difficult, if not impossible, to imagine the great railroad barons playing toy trains with their infant progeny. These were busy fathers, of whom sensitivity was not required, men whose parental obligation was viewed as the provision not of playthings but of legacies. Gifts to young children were solemn and purposeful: a Parisian-dressed doll too beautiful to touch, an exquisite replica of father's coach-and-four. There was the mink coverlet that Madeleine Astor presented to her infant son, John Jacob VI; the strand of seed pearls Alice Vanderbilt presented to her daughter on her twelfth birthday to launch her debut at society teas; the rifle given to the frail Teddy Roosevelt by his father when Teddy turned thirteen in the hope of deflecting his attention from books to more manly outdoor pursuits.

At the age of fifteen, Dorothy Fritz received from her father, Eugene Fritz, the ponderous gift of San Francisco's Huntington Hotel. For her coming out, the daughter of Mrs. Horace Dodge received from her mother an eight-hundred-thousand-dollar pearl necklace that had belonged to Catherine the Great.

Occasionally, a ray of light shone through. Alice Roosevelt Longworth, Teddy's daughter, wrote charmingly of a dollhouse "given to me when I was about six by my Grandfather Lee, and I have added considerably to its furniture over the years. I enjoy rearranging it to this day." But for the most part, the houses received by her playmates were very much larger—and bestowed only upon marriage.

The tradition of giving real estate to one's child dates back to America's formative days. To the west, the Spanish land grant island of Coronado was her father's munificent wedding gift to Caroline Sepulveda. To the east, the spacious Woodlawn estate, two thousand acres of his Mount Vernon plantation, was given by George Washington to his adopted daughter, Nelly, when she married his nephew in 1799. Washington then undertook construction of a red-brick Georgian mansion for the young couple that took five years to complete, by which time both the President and Martha had died.

Space looms larger in Texas, and in the late 1800s cattle baron Captain Richard King owned a good deal of the southern portion of it. Lest the forty thousand acres he and his wife Henrietta deeded to their son on his marriage seem insignificant by comparison, the Kings built for the young couple a spacious colonnaded mansion, La Puerta de Agua Dulce, which continues to preside over what still constitutes the largest private ranch in America.

By the turn of the century, as wealth increasingly defined society, so key was one's dwelling to the determination of one's status that it became *de rigueur* to start one's child off in marriage with the accustomed roof overhead. When he married Adele Neustadt and received 932 Fifth Avenue from his father, Mortimer Schiff gratefully acknowledged, "It's nice to own a house in which I got so many spankings." Darius O. Mills, the mining and railroad tycoon, displaced himself into a virtual palace opposite St. Patrick's Cathedral when his daughter married Whitelaw Reid, conferring upon her his Villard mansion.

For her wedding present, Mary Harkness was given the sumptuous mansion at 1 East Seventy-fifth Street, the present Harkness House. When Caroline Astor commissioned a block-long residence from Richard Morris Hunt, she asked him to design it in two parts so that she could give half to her son, John Jacob IV. So mutually pleased with the union of Gertrude Vanderbilt and Harry Payne Whitney were their respective fathers that they vied with each other as to which would provide the residence. Mrs. Vanderbilt neatly resolved the dilemma in a note to her daughter: "Yesterday I received a letter from Mr. Whitney telling us that he intended giving Harry his house . . . I wrote to Mr. Whitney that your father told you that he would give you a house . . . as that plan is now spoiled he must at least let your father furnish it."

When they had no status mansions to spare, indulgent fathers created them. For his daughter Marjorie Merriweather's first marriage, cereal king C.W. Post built The Boulders in Greenwich, Connecticut, which boasted the longest porch in the history of architecture. Daniel Guggenheim gave his son and his new daughter-in-law substantial acreage at Sands Point, Long Island, building for them the magnificent thirty-room Falaise; it took Harry and Caroline two years of travel around

Europe to gather all the furnishings and works of art. Three thousand miles to the west, Edward Doheny (of Teapot Dome notoriety) was siphoning four million dollars from his seventy-five-million-dollar oil fortune to build Greystone, an English manor house with an Olympic-size pool, two lakes, two bowling alleys, and a seven-room gatehouse—which hardly added up to your average dwelling, even in Beverly Hills.

But then, these were not average fathers. They were the possessors of colossal new fortunes, the titans of railroads and oil and banking and steel. These were men quarried, not born—men attuned above all to the hard clink of millions, which, in those tax-free days, were passed on virtually intact to their children: to daughters who bought titled husbands across the Atlantic, to sons who measured success in the trebling of those millions, to daughters-in-law who moved from triumph to triumph in their Worth gowns and Medici jewels, past the liveried servants, addresses on Fifth Avenue, Pullman cars, yachts, boxes at the opera, and annual balls, into the eye of the social cyclone—and immortality in the Social Register.

From this haven, their grandchildren rollicked into the twenties as the Fast Set: spoiled scions who, as Henry James put it, could stand a good deal of gold; pampered heiresses who were offered whatever they coveted, who were brought up to expect that all oysters hold pearls, who never learned to say, "Darling, you shouldn't have." These were F. Scott Fitzgerald's rich rich, who moved carelessly from the right club to the nightclub, secure in the belief there was no one wealthier than their fathers.

The fallout from an age in which the only prohibition was liquor was predictably calamitous, as fathers with too much to give ruined their children with hazardous racing cars, disastrous marriages, and an excess of property and jewelry. The flower of society's youth might have succumbed altogether had it not been for the Great Depression and World War II, which banished nurseries and their attendant governesses and, together with the new psychology, taught the value of intimacy.

The new parents interacted with their children, writing a different sort of social record—one that documents a desire to share, an eagerness to listen, and a longing to create for the child the world of fantasy and fun that the parents never had. There were occasional throwbacks to that feckless time when Evalyn Walsh McLean had only to stamp her

GUILFORD DUDLEY JR.
To
TREVANIA DUDLEY

Above, Dudley's Lady in Lace.

Vincente Minnelli To Liza Minnelli

Above, Liza Minnelli in costume.

ten-year-old foot to obtain from her father, in order to save her walking to school, a blue-and-silver victoria led by a pair of sorrels and a coachman in a top hat. She herself would give her son, Vinson, a diminutive coach (its coverlet matching the ermine suit she had Worth design for him) and three miniature horses. The Pullman car that Barbara Hutton wheedled out of Grandfather Woolworth was not exactly a toy. Nor was the railroad in Texas which New York's eccentric millionaire Hetty Green gave her son Ned so that he might run it back and forth at whim along the whole two hundred miles, with no stops and no passengers.

But, for the most part, even profligate parents had learned that the yellow-brick roads of their childrens' universe were paved largely with time and imagination. The new parents created fantasy playlands. Comedian Harold Lloyd built a miniature playhouse for his three children, personally supervising details of plumbing and electricity, and installing such elaborate furnishings that his daughter Gloria begged for a lock so she could secure it at night. Vincente Minnelli commissioned scaled-down versions of the prettiest costumes from MGM films so that Liza could have the dress-up parties of her dreams.

The new parents listened. One spring, when Howard Hughes was a shy fourteen, his father took him to a Harvard-Yale football game and promised that if Harvard won he would give his son anything he desired. Harvard did win and Howard could have asked for the earth, but the only thing he wanted was a ride in the seaplane he had seen moored in the Charles. Not without some difficulty, his father honored his word—triggering a fantasy that would be realized many years and millions of dollars later when Hughes defied gravity with his prodigious *Spruce Goose.*

The new parents invested time in their children. It was not the splendor of the costly electric train his father gave him for his birthday that is best remembered by Michael Spock, son of the celebrated pediatrician; it is the many hours they spent building its platform and manning it together. Former Ambassador to Denmark Guilford Dudley has taken time from his busy schedule to paint a portrait of his daughter, Trevania, every Christmas of her life.

The new parents waved the magic wand. Television mogul Aaron Spelling and his wife, Candy, would spread rare seashells along the beach so their infant daughter could discover them. For her fifth birthday, they imported truckloads of snow to simulate a winter she had never seen. For her tenth birthday dance, Tori's request for the music of Michael Jackson was met with the appearance of Michael Jackson himself.

Parental generosity followed children into adulthood. His daughter Kitty was already Mrs. Gilbert Miller when Jules Bache gave her the painting she coveted, Goya's *Red Boy*. Knowing that his son swam regularly to relieve the pain in his back, Joseph P. Kennedy commissioned a mural to enhance the White House pool.

With the passing of years and the passing along of fortunes, the roles were often reversed, the children becoming the donors and the parents the grateful recipients. That most treasured drawing affixed to the fridge with a magnet and that first clay pot brought home from school beribboned in yarn evolved into gifts of a more extravagant nature.

It was her daughter Eleanor who capped Marjorie Post's already priceless collection of Fabergé with the last great Easter Egg, which had been made in 1914 as a Christmas present from Czar Nicholas II to his mother. It was his son Edsel who had Tiffany send around to Henry Ford, on the occasion of his birthday, a three-hundred-thousand-dollar collection of silver. Aiming at a more striking presentation for his father's sixty-fifth birthday, the banker and art collector Robert Lehman placed a diminutive Botticelli painting under a layer of chocolates in a nondescript box and watched with anticipation for the moment of discovery as the confection was passed around the banquet table.

More sentimental, perhaps, are sons' presents to their mothers. Young Teddy Roosevelt concocted a necklace from the claws of the first tiger he felled and mailed it to his mother from Hyderabad. When Elvis Presley made his first hit record, he bought for his mother the pink Cadillac she had always longed for. In a deep gesture of affection for his Aunt Marie, Truman Capote, at the age of twenty-one, wrote the 7,500-word novella *Cousin Bud*. She must have valued it highly, since she squirreled it away in a brown paper bag, which she stumbled across in the attic while researching family history at the time of the author's death. "I read it and loved it and just kept it as something Truman had given me."

JOSEPH P. KENNEDY
To
JOHN F. KENNEDY

Above, the White House mural.

Oscar Hammerstein II was composer and lyricist Stephen Sondheim's mentor. Sondheim's parents introduced him to Hammerstein when Sondheim was a boy.

"At the age of eleven," recalls Dorothy Hammerstein, "Stephen taught Oscar how to play chess. Stephen has always loved games and so I decided to give him a chess set that belonged to Oscar and that was originally made for King Charles II."

Through the years, Stephen Sondheim has put to work what Hammerstein taught him in such great musical successes as *Company, Sweeney Todd* and *Sunday in the Park with George.* He maintains his love for chess, and he has devised other games in the form of puzzles as gifts for his friends.

Above, Stephen Sondheim.

S. Dillon Ripley, former Secretary of the Smithsonian Institution: "One evening in the late 1950s, my friend James Babb, Librarian of Yale University, came over with his wife to have coffee with my wife and me. 'Dillon,' he said, 'I have a present for your daughter, Julie, and I think it has the kind of association that might amuse her.' And he produced this box, made out of many richly colored woods. 'Years ago,' he explained, 'one of your relatives gave it to the Yale Library.' He opened it up, and inside was written: 'Made from the railroad car which transported Abraham Lincoln's remains on the famous train trip from Washington through various cities, ending up in Spring-field, Illinois, where he is buried.'

"The box had been made from the wood of the car, which had been provided by my great-grandfather, Sydney Dillon, who at the time of Lincoln's death was a vice president of the Union Pacific Railroad. After the ceremonies and the funeral, the car was broken up. He had given the box to his daughter, my grandmother, Julie Dillon. 'That is why,' Jim Babb said, 'I would like you to have it for your Julie, and it is better off back in the Ripley family.'"

In 1945, master wood-carver and sculptor Alphons Weber took his four-year-old grandniece, Carolyn, to see the Colleen Moore Dollhouse, in Chicago's Museum of Science and Industry, which he had worked on years before. Carolyn was fascinated and asked Weber (who had done the carvings for the Thorne miniature rooms at the Art Institute of Chicago and displays for Marshall Field's) if he could make her a little something, too.

Weber spent many evenings piecing together for her this elaborate castle. Modeled after one in his native Germany, it is crafted of oatmeal tins and cigar boxes and was, appropriately enough, completed on Weber's kitchen table.

Above left, Alphons Weber's grandniece.

Lyda Bunker Hunt
To
Caroline Hunt Schoellkopf

Caroline Hunt Schoellkopf, daughter of H.L. Hunt, says that her most treasured gift, from her mother, came to her completely unexpectedly. "My mother and I had gone to New York together, where we had attended an antique show at the Armory. We were sitting at the airport waiting for our plane home when I accidentally kicked over her purchase, a beautiful cranberry-glass vase.

"The vase was broken and I was terribly upset, but my mother said it was all right, she had so much cranberry anyway. I kept apologizing and saying how much I loved her cranberry collection. Suddenly she said, 'If you like it that much, it's yours.'

"Though she gave it to me right there and then, it looked so pretty displayed in her window over the stairway with the sunlight shining through it that I left it there until after her death. Now I have it on exhibit in the dining room of The Mansion on Turtle Creek, where everyone can enjoy it as much as I do.

"The reason this gift means so much to me is that it is a reminder of my mother's forgiving and generous nature. The ultimate gift that any person is able to give another is sharing the person that he or she is."

Above, Lyda Bunker Hunt and Caroline Hunt Schoellkopf.

Above, right, names of children who have used the crib.

Dinah Shore, Melissa's mother: "When I was carrying our first child, my husband made a crib out of maple and pine. He was a very good craftsman, but this was beyond anything he had attempted before. He carved all the animals that were specific to his native state, Montana, and mine, Tennessee. On the back he carved the date, 1948.

"It was such a fine welcoming for our first-born. When we brought Melissa home—it's the happiest time of your life anyway—I dissolved. The crib was used many times again: by our son, John, by Deborah Kerr, by the Edgar Bergens, and now by our grandchildren."

80

Dorothy Rodgers: "My niece made this miniature bookcase for me. She made every book. First she photographed them and then reduced the photographs. There is the Rodgers and Hart songbook and a Rodgers and Hammerstein songbook, and then all of my books, and my husband's autobiography, and books written by our friends. Below are the album covers, photographed front and back. Look at all the time she put into it—the titles, the little flowers. Margot gave it to me for Christmas 1982 and I absolutely adore it."

At the age of eighteen, immediately after graduating from prep school, Vice President George Bush volunteered for the Navy Reserve. He was sworn in as the youngest carrier pilot to be commissioned.

As a tribute and a talisman, his proud parents gave him these gold cuff links. They are engraved with his initials and embossed with platinum Navy wings. The cuff links saw him safely through heavy action, marking a war record that, while Bush treats it lightly, was a distinguished one.

"I was shot down in the Pacific at age twenty. I am not sure that is the best credential for a vice-presidential candidate, but that was my first government job and it imbued in me the ideal of service."

Above, George Bush at age eighteen.

Her Children
To
Elizabeth Folger Miller Cooper

Vilmos Gabor
To
Zsa Zsa Gabor

San Francisco civic leader Betty Cooper: "For Christmas 1963, I received from all my children what they call a grandmother's pin, which my daughter Marion Miller designed. The idea was that each time a grandchild was born, another of the spaces would be filled with a precious stone—rubies for the granddaughters, sapphires for the grandsons, and, eventually, diamonds for the great-grandchildren.

"When I received it there were only a few stones, but now I have thirty-three grandchildren and thirteen great-grandchildren, so there are only a few spaces left."

Zsa Zsa Gabor: "Darling, my most favorite gift of all is this. I last saw my father fifteen years ago in Vienna. He had come from Budapest to see us all (my mother and my two sisters). As we said goodby, he took me aside and pulled this diamond tiara out of his pocket: 'I want you to have this,' he said. He was a jeweler and the communists had taken everything he had, but somehow he had saved this.

"I took it apart and made a big diamond crown. I wear it quite often in Palm Beach and everyone comments on it. That is the best present."

Actor Roddy McDowall has not always played such mature roles as Mordred in *Camelot*. His film days go back to the tender age of eight in England. His Hollywood days began at age twelve, when Darryl F. Zanuck brought him, accompanied by his mother, to America and Twentieth Century Fox. *How Green Was My Valley* endeared him to Americans, and the love affair continued with *My Friend Flicka* and *Lassie Come Home.*

Among his memories of those first years in Hollywood is the following, of a gift from a boyhood hero.

Roddy McDowall: "When I was a small child, under contract to Twentieth Century Fox, Laurel and Hardy were making their films there. I loved them—what child didn't?

"I used to haunt their sets. One of the biggest thrills of my young life was when Stan took off his hat one day and inscribed the sweatband to me and put it on my head. It was a lovely gesture and I have remembered it always."

Above, Roddy McDowall.

DAVID NIVEN JR

NOEL COWARD *To* DAVID NIVEN, JR.

Noel Coward and David Niven were close friends as well as kindred spirits—both of them gentlemen, both debonair figures in a world of paparazzi and glitz. When David, Jr., was born, it was a foregone conclusion that Coward would be the godfather. More conjectural was what gift Coward, unfamiliar as he was with the world of rattles, would take to the christening. He wanted something that would be suitable yet not insufferably dull.

At Asprey's in London, he found just the thing: a cocktail shaker guaranteed, some years later, to mix a fine-tasting formula. Coward's inscription in his own handwriting: "Because, my godson dear, I rather think you will grow up like your father. My gift is this and with it given a toast: fine health to Master Niven. May all gay things on you be showered today and always.—Noel Coward."

David is enthralled with the gift, but he says, "My father got a lot more use out of it than I."

THE GIFT FOR AN

Occasion

EMPRESS OF CHINA
To
ALICE ROOSEVELT

Above, Alice and her dog.

*S*ave the wedding presents!" The cry echoed down the corridors at the nuptials of steel magnate James Farrell's daughter and the eldest son of Thomas E. Murray of Southampton. A fire had broken out in the midst of the celebrations, and concerned guests sounded the alarm, anticipating puddles of vermeil where only moments before they had passed in admiration before the glittering evidence of their own generosity. With supreme unconcern, their jovial host moved the festivities outdoors and ordered the glasses refilled. As the champagne flowed like water, the wedding presents flowed like lava. "It's all right," insisted the father of the bride. "Don't worry, it's all insured."

His composure was warranted. The stuff of obligation—silver spoons and gilded tea sets from Tiffany or Cartier—is easily replaced. Its function in society, however, is not. The obligatory gift exchange dictated by convention comes so close to reducing the gift to mere product that it calls into question the meaning of giving itself. The conventional transaction is not a voluntary one: the giver must give, the receiver must reciprocate. Those who take part in the gift exchange are bound together by the ritual in alliances of political, economic, or social expedience. Most spectacular of such rituals were the great potlatch ceremonies of the American Northwest Indians, at which the Kwakiutl gave away or destroyed valuable possessions in order to demonstrate their wealth and their right to high rank. However, the meeting of any two great estates invariably engenders ceremonial exchange.

In the society of nations, gift exchange is the glue of diplomacy, creating new ties and patching eroding ones. Oddly in contrast to our propensity for panache, America's official giving has been markedly restrained. We have not approached the largesse of the Dowager Empress of China, who bestowed so many gifts upon President Theodore Roosevelt's daughter, Alice, that her visit to Peking was referred to as "Alice in Plunderland." We have not paralleled the prodigality of France's gift to Mrs. Woodrow Wilson, who had been alerted to the arrival of a tapestry and made room for a throw rug, only to be overwhelmed by an eighteen-foot Gobelin masterwork. We have not touched the hem of our great Statue of Liberty, the spontaneous gift of the people of France, who in 1886 raised two hundred fifty thousand dollars to construct such a substantial testimony to their friendship for us that it required more than two hundred crates to get it across the Atlantic. We have barely matched the graciousness of Premier Nikita Khrushchev, who despite his well-aired differences with President Kennedy presented him with a model of an American whaler carved from whalebone, an example of an art form he knew the President collected.

We are, of course, a democracy and may wish to project ourselves as a plain-speaking people. Certainly the tokens of our diplomatic esteem have been, if tasteful, remarkably low-key. Steuben bowls have been standard: Truman gave one to Princess Elizabeth of England on the occasion of her marriage, and President Reagan gave another to mark the wedding of Princess Diana and Prince Charles. President Kennedy preferred ship models and rare books but went to an extreme for Pope Paul VI, for whom he asked the First Lady to design a vermeil correspondence case. Lyndon Johnson liked silver: he took an engraver along on his travels, together with an assortment of boxes and bowls, inscribing them to new political allies as he passed through. For Pope Paul VI he too went all out, ordering a one-of-a-kind Tiffany item, a three-inch vermeil globe of the world. Richard Nixon's taste ran to Boehm: a magnificent pair of porcelain swans, signifying peace (they took two years to make) extended our goodwill to Chairman Mao. Nixon bordered on the extravagant when he presented Japan's Premier Sato with a model of the White House fashioned by jeweler David Webb out of fourteen-carat gold.

Gifts of state might have swelled into a reasonable facsimile of largesse had it not been for the Foreign Gifts Act of 1956, which made it unlawful to transfer presents from abroad worth over fifty dollars to the President's personal use. It was somewhat loosely observed by succeeding administrations until Ford set the tone for literal adherence by restricting the nation's liberality to an eight-by-ten photograph. Even the Shah of Iran, who had enriched the White House with more than one priceless carpet, on his last official visit to Washington received only a glossy likeness of the President. Happily the Reagans, refusing to compromise their *savoir faire*, sent a personal present for the birth of Prince William: a corner Chippendale child's chair upholstered in needlepoint (similar to a pair that had been given to their own children). Lest even personal generosity be misconstrued by the press, the White House was careful to make clear that the chair was a reproduction.

JEAN JUSSERAND To EDITH BOLLING WILSON

Above, Wilson's Gobelin tapestry.

RONALD AND NANCY REAGAN
To
PRINCE WILLIAM

Below, the child's chair given to Prince William.

Above, Boehm swans given to Mao.

RICHARD NIXON
To
MAO TSE-TUNG

That restraint is a strain on the American character can be seen from our profligacy in private matters of protocol and our obvious relish for domestic ceremonies. Polite society has rejected the potlatch but produced the party, a concomitant of conspicuous prosperity that evolved in the space of two decades into a cultural spectacle designed to gift friends with a night to remember. What some of America's new rich spent on one party might have supported a family of five in comfort for a lifetime. The Sharon-Newlands wedding reception made headlines in the *San Francisco Chronicle:* "Two thousand dollars to decorate each window," they marveled, "or the cost of a cozy cottage in Oakland."

By the turn of the century, the party had become the supreme toy of the privileged class, as the overnight tycoons, whom Steinbeck called "at once our curse and our ornament," confected out of a ceremonial obligation the stagiest party of them all, a supreme public presentation of wealth and power served on a bed of a thousand orchids. Literal fortunes were spent on trimmings not meant to outlast the dawn: three thousand roses tied to the trees for the wedding of Virginia Fair to William K. Vanderbilt II, five thousand chrysanthemums dyed pink for Marjorie Post's marriage to Joseph Davies, two thousand cases of champagne for one thousand guests at the debut of Barbara Hutton. "That was a party," recalled Evalyn Walsh McLean of one of her Washington extravaganzas. "There were forty-eight for dinner, and the cost of the entertainment was forty thousand dollars; much of that was for orchids and for four thousand two-dollar yellow lilies, brought from London." She was nothing if not the true daughter of mining king Thomas Walsh, that great giver of cotillions, who readily admitted to a fondness for spectacle: "It is only when the thing I buy creates a show for those around me that I get my money's worth."

It was essential, of course, that the show not be forgotten. To engrave the gift of the party upon the memory of its recipients, a present within the present was devised, a tangible keepsake in the form of a party favor. Walsh himself liked his guests to make their selection from a table piled high with gold pencils and tortoiseshell fans. Diamond Jim Brady once spent over a hundred thousand nineteenth-century dollars on a dinner for fifty, more than half of it for the diamond brooches and diamond-studded stopwatches served to his guests on red-velvet cushions. Leonard Jerome, grandfather of Winston Churchill, was renowned in Edwardian New York as an unparalleled host; he bestowed on each lady at one banquet at Delmonico's a substantial gold bracelet. Alice-of-The-Breakers Vanderbilt liked to upstage her sister-in-law's conventional silver party favors with trinkets of eighteen-carat gold. However, Alva outdid Alice and even herself at the Newport party she gave for her daughter's intended, the ninth Duke of Marlborough, for which she had gleaned from the Faubourg St. Honoré five thousand dollars' worth of favors from the time of Louis XI—etchings, fans, mirrors, and watchcases, each tagged with a medallion embossed with a likeness of Marble House.

Since Newport was the most visible of the battlegrounds for social supremacy, as party countered party so did favor outdo favor. At one event, cigars were wrapped in hundred-dollar bills. At another, the centerpiece was a sand hill and each setting had a little silver pail and shovel with which guests scooped up buried gems.

Naturally, the old guard professed themselves immune to such vulgar bids for entrée. When one parvenu reportedly invited fifty of the establishment for dinner, only twenty showed up. Under each napkin, the tolerant few found a gold cigarette case or a mesh purse embedded with diamonds. Next morning, the town buzzed about the bad taste of such bribery. However, when the hostess entertained again, she invited sixty to dinner—and seventy turned up.

Meanwhile, Manhattan, never impractical in material matters, danced merrily to the band music of ever-escalating favors, reaching a pinnacle at the Mayflower Hotel on Christmas Day, 1926, the eve of Helen Doherty's debut. At a dinner for twelve intimates, the oil magnate's daughter presented each with a Ford Cabriolet, hand-decorated with hunting scenes, and expedited a thirteenth to an absent friend, the King of Spain.

Even Barbara Hutton's wedding favors did not outclass these, though she herself made a staggering haul: half a dozen diamond bracelets, several gold vanity cases, multiples of Baccarat, and enough Georgian flatware to dine five hundred at one sitting.

A wedding, of course, was the ultimate potlatch. It was the last spin of the wheel, when the father of the bride called in all the chips—and in the gambling halls of the plutocracy the chips were piled high. The House of Rothschild must have owed no small debt to their representative, August Belmont, to have bestowed on his son's bride a brooch set with a diamond that the press called "overwhelming." When William K. Vanderbilt's daughter was married, the gifts his friends sent commandeered three salons merely for storage, with an additional two for display. That there were business points to be gained from a gift relationship with Henry Ford II was evidenced on the occasion of his son's marriage to Anne McDonnell, at which sixteen guards were assigned to the wedding presents. His own gift to the couple was a custom-built Ford complete with chauffeur—who, presumably, stood his own guard.

The obligation to do well by one's own, reflected in the dowry, reached its zenith in America's Gilded Age. "If she's good enough for you, she's good enough for me," was Waldorf Astor's prelude to gifting his son's bride, Nancy Langhorne, with the legendary Sancy diamond.

The Comstock Lode's bonanza king, James Fair, preferred to send his daughter into the world with more liquid assets, namely one million dollars, which Theresa instantly translated into a Newport estate upon which there arose, at Stanford White's behest, a close imitation of the Grand Trianon.

Since it cannot have been inflation, it must have been the title that stimulated the notedly frugal tycoon Collis P. Huntington to raise the going dowry by two million when his daughter, Clara, became Princess Von Hatzfeld-Wildenberg. The title was expressly the reason Alva Vanderbilt gave her daughter the celebrated pearls of Catherine the Great on the occasion of her marriage to the Duke of Marlborough—the closest an American heiress would come to royalty. "I forced her to marry the Duke," Alva readily testified. Although William was less eager for his daughter's unhappiness, he came through with a diamond tiara for Consuelo, two and a half million dollars' worth of railroad stock for the Duke, and a hundred-thousand-dollar annual allowance for each.

Anna Gould picked her own title, which was quite genuine but not one the family approved of. Fiancé Boni de Castellane's tastes ran to Rembrandts, which boded ill for the Gould fortune. Nevertheless, protocol was observed, eliciting from her relatives a necklace of eight hundred pearls, a chain of two hundred diamonds, a silver dinner service inlaid with rubies, and a diamond coronet. After Boni duly went through twelve million Gould dollars subsidizing the purveyors of the Rue de la Paix, Anna divorced him and then married their

CLARENCE MACKAY
To
ANNA CASE

JOHNNY ENGSTEAD
To
MAX SHOWALTER

Below, Anna Case's emeralds.

Below, Carole Lombard in her dining room.

Above, balloon pottery.

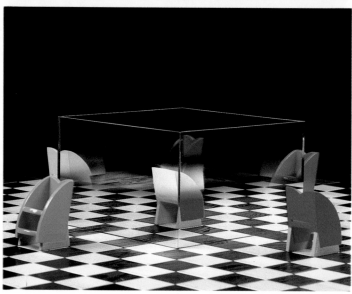

Above, Bell's Chairs in Space.

PAIGE RENSE
To
MALCOLM AND ROBERTA FORBES

LARRY BELL
To
THURSTON AND LILA TWIGG-SMITH

neighbor, who, through the niceties of French genealogy, was both a marquis and a duke. For this second ceremony, perhaps on the assumption that one coronet can serve in two crownings, the family held back.

Although the only exchange prescribed between the bridal couple is a wedding band, custom has carved expectations as big as the Ritz. Or, at the least, emeralds "the size of an egg," as Cartier described the matchless necklace, now lighting up the Smithsonian, which mining king Clarence Mackay gave opera singer Anna Case on the occasion of their marriage.

A string of polo ponies, a mansion, several sports cars, a converted B-25 and five hundred thousand dollars in cash were all wedding presents from Doris Duke to Porfirio Rubirosa. They signed a prenuptial agreement, a type of document whose increasing proliferation has come to signify most strongly the contractual nature of the obligatory gift.

Barbara Hutton's bridal gifts to her seven husbands were equally lavish. (Polo ponies must have been *de rigueur,* since both Mdivani and Rubirosa received them.) Her divorce gifts were better publicized, hovering (depending on who pressed hardest) between the two million to Mdivani and the three million to Haugwitz-Reventlow. Only Cary Grant bowed out like a gentleman, in the civilized belief that there are occasions in life when it is better to leave than to receive.

The divorce present, that newest arrival on the roster of requisite giving, was a fitting valedictory for a dying era. Two world wars and a depression drove ostentation underground. Hollywood took up the banner for a brief if well-recorded interval when hills were covered in camellias, champagne flowed from fountains, and swimming pools were filled with Chanel No. 5—until stockholders intervened and put an end to the movie studios' largesse. Hollywood's grandest events are now charity functions, where the only favors are product samples and the centerpieces that the more intrepid march off with.

Even Texas entertaining has toned down since Everett de Golyer of Dallas, the collector of railroad trains, asked Neiman's to select fifty-cent favors for his millionaires' lunches. Stanley Marcus recalls that wrapping the gifts cost easily twice that.

With the great public profferings of wealth and prodigality gone to cover, America's by now highly developed habit of obligatory giving has surfaced in the ever-increasing number of personal events we deem it necessary to acknowledge by a token. Births, christenings, bar mitzvahs, engagements, weddings, and anniversaries—all constitute significant events in the American life cycle. Whether as arbitrary as a housewarming or as inevitable as Christmas, each implies a present as a bride does a groom.

The resultant panic is predictable. The birthday alone, an American institution regarded with some wonder by the rest of the world, presents itself as a perennial problem seeking an annual solution. The talented among us rise to the challenge with grace and imagination, shopping throughout the year for something appropriate to a friend or an occasion. Such was the set of pottery with balloon motifs that *Architectural Digest*'s Paige Rense ferreted out to thank the Malcolm Forbeses, who own the world's first ballooning museum, for a delightful weekend in their chateau near Deauville. The rest of us thank our lucky stars for the gift catalogue and the local florist. Few any longer are reduced to the straits of FDR, who once found himself enclosing a birthday check in a letter to his wife, Eleanor, along with protestations of helplessness.

The readiest solution is giving a gift you would like for yourself. One Christmas, Edward Boehm presented his bemused wife with four Jersey heifers. They were not exactly what Helen had in mind; what she really wanted was a stunning malachite clock—which she had conveniently purchased as her gift to Edward.

At times the gift is made long before the occasion to present it arises. When actor Max Showalter bought a home on Hollywood Boulevard, his friend photographer Johnny Engstead presented him with the perfect housewarming gift. In Engstead's files was a series of photographs he had taken years before of one of the house's former occupants— Carole Lombard. The photos had never been published and provide glimpses of the house's interior, itself a gift to Lombard from decorator Billy Haines.

Once again the artist holds the trump card. When artist Larry Bell accepted the Twigg-Smiths' offer to vacation in their house on Oahu, he sent them as a thank-you gift the complex new work *Chairs in Space,* which the collectors had just trekked to his Taos studio to view.

King Hassan II of Morocco
To
Princess Lee Radziwill

Lee Radziwill: "In 1963, I went to Marrakesh with my sister as guest of King Hassan II. Every year at that time, the King visits Marrakesh to watch the Fantasia, which is the most colorful event imaginable, when the Berber tribesmen come down from the Atlas Mountains on their magnificent Arab stallions to pay tribute to their King. At one point, I commented to the King on a particularly magnificent white horse which had just passed.

"When I returned to the Bahia Palace, I had an unexpected visit from the King's elder sister, Princess Lalla Aisha, who asked me to come down to the courtyard. There in the sun stood the superb white Arab stallion I had so much admired. Standing at his side was his owner, the Governor of Marrakesh. He smiled and said how honored he was to present me with what I knew must be his greatest treasure. I knew I had to accept, although for his sake I was heartbroken.

"Later I asked the head groom how he thought the horse would manage in England, where I lived. He said, 'If it is very sandy there, he will do fine.' My heart sank.

"I decided to board the stallion locally until an appropriate amount of time had passed, then I wrote to the King's brother that I felt the horse should be returned to his original owner as I could not care for him properly. I visited him once briefly two years later, on a trip to Morocco with my husband, and that was the last I ever saw or heard of him.

"However, I shall never forget the drama and the beauty of the presentation to me of that maginificent white stallion in that ravishing pink city."

Above, Lee Radziwill.

97

Frances Elkins
To
Tony and Beegle Duquette

When artist Tony Duquette and his wife Beegle were married in 1949 at the legendary Pickfair, they received many wonderful gifts. Still proudly displayed in the Duquette home is this pair of sixteenth-century Venetian dolphins. They were a gift from the influential California decorator Frances Elkins.

The dolphins had once belonged to Misia Sert, and Elkins felt their flowing lines would serve as inspiration for Duquette's art as well as ornament for his home. In fact, Duquette once removed them from their honored places near the sofa to use them in the decor of an exhibit of his works.

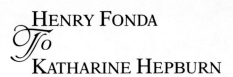

HENRY FONDA
To
KATHARINE HEPBURN

Two giant stars of the cinema, Katharine Hepburn and Henry Fonda, had never met until cast together in *On Golden Pond*—a pairing that proved magical. Fonda recalled: "The very first day she came up to me, holding something in her outstretched hands. 'I want you to have this,' she said to me. 'This was Spencer's favorite hat.' What a gracious thing to do. It was the exact hat that John Ford wore while he directed pictures. And I knew that Ford and Spencer had been close friends, hard drinking Irishmen. It was Ford's good luck hat. I was thrilled with it. I put it on and Katharine nodded, and I wore it in the first scene we shot that day.

"While we were making the picture, Katharine asked me to do a painting for her, sort of a memento of our working together. I was very flattered that she wanted a painting of mine. I promised her one because I consider her someone very rare but I didn't have the faintest notion of what the subject should be. Then, a week after we returned home to California, my costumes arrived. I opened the overstuffed box and three objects tumbled out. Right then and there I knew exactly what to do for Katharine."

Fonda simply lined up his three favorite hats: on the right his tan fishing hat, in the middle his rain hat, and on the left the battered brown felt hat that had belonged to Spencer Tracy.

THE GIFT OF

Appreciation

CHARLES WARD
To
FRANKLIN ROOSEVELT

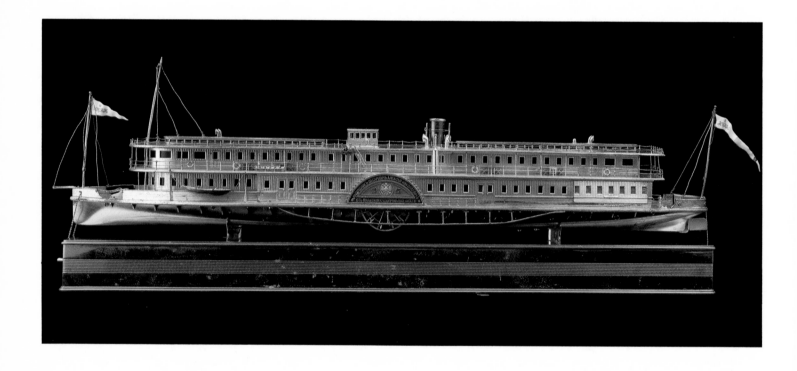

Above, FDR's Fabergé paddle steamer.

*N*othing—not George Washington's cherry tree, not Lincoln's Gettysburg Address—pulled at America's heartstrings as did Charles Lindbergh's nonstop flight across the Atlantic that May of 1927. With the Lone Eagle soared the spirit of the nation, which showered its hero with a ticker-tape of presents, from egg warmers crocheted by Minnesota housewives to a pair of eighteenth-century silver globes from William Randolph Hearst. Towns, streets, even babies were named Lindbergh. At the parade staged in the hero's honor, New York's flamboyant mayor, Jimmy Walker, surpassed even himself: "Colonel Lindbergh, New York City is yours. I give it to you." No one thought the gesture excessive.

When a job is done and is done well, a handshake is not enough. For service beyond the call of duty, a thank-you letter is inadequate. For that extra team effort, that pull on the oar, that score on the field, the appreciative colleague longs to reinforce the pat on the back with a tangible tribute. At the level of commerce the reward is a bonus; at the level of patriotism it is a medal. But at the level of community and neighborhood, at all those crossroads where lives intersect and interacting talents and efforts create a heightened mutuality, heartfelt gratitude seeks more personal expression.

At its most basic, the gift of appreciation is for services well rendered. "What can I get you for Christmas?" Moss Hart asked his superagent, Irving "Swifty" Lazar, who had lived up to his name in brisk deals for the producer. No slouch at repartee, Swifty, long desirous of adding that star to his firmament, shot back, "Get me Cole Porter." "Done," replied Hart, and it was.

At its most spectacular, the gift of gratitude is for the life saved. In the case of Charles Ward it was his reputation, which amounted to the same thing. He had been jailed in 1920 for violation of the narcotics laws, paroled five years later, and in the following decade had risen to a financial position of some consequence. In 1935, FDR granted him an official pardon. So grateful was Ward for the restoration of his rights as a citizen that he gifted the President with a Fabergé presentation model of a paddle steamer.

In a more literal rescue, effected at the opening of New York's restaurant The Passy, someone dropped ashes on Paulette Goddard's dress. As the organdy went up like a torch, Frances Cheney, better known as "Froggy," but not at all known for her cool, pushed her flaming friend down the staircase, rolling her in its carpet until the flames were extinguished. A few weeks later, Froggy received from the survivor a massive diamond brooch in the shape of a fireman's helmet.

Fire was also the occasion of panic at Vincent Price's home. It was New Year's Eve and some of old-guard Hollywood were gathered for festivities at the abode of the master of the macabre when the whole of Bel Air caught fire. As the flames crept closer, the guests rolled up their cuff links, loaded their Cadillacs with fine art, dumped the silver in the pool, and continued to perform all manner of rescue operations until the flames licked at the neighboring house and Price urged his friends to drive themselves and his treasures to safety. What the fleeing squirrels might have thought had they recognized Edward G. Robinson in black tie heading south with ten masterpieces was never reported. But all Hollywood was abuzz with the next morning's activities, as the revelers returned clad in the era's equivalent of jeans to work through the day at putting everything back in place. Vincent Price matched his gratitude to their efforts, gifting each savior with a choice morsel from his collection. The Peruvian *santos* that Bill Frye received still graces his atrium, "protecting my house and greeting me when I come home."

Equally cherished is the glass screen painted by the French artist Drian with a likeness of her good friend and great beauty of the period Audrey Pleydell-Bouverie, which fashion publicist Eleanor Lambert rescued not from a fire but from oblivion. Hearing, after her friend's death, that her estate was being auctioned, Eleanor sent word to Audrey's son, Jeremy James, that she would like to buy the screen by private treaty. Touched, he sent it to her as a gift.

At its most poignant, the gift of esteem is that passed along to the next generation. In a gesture of magical significance, the celebrated illusionist Harry Keller presented his already famous protégé, Houdini, with his psychomachine, an enigmatic contrivance with which he had created his best-known illusions. The great jazz musician Louis Armstrong was in his teens when he received his most meaningful accolade, from jazz master Joe Oliver. "It was my ambition to play as he did. I still think if it had not been for Joe Oliver, jazz would not be what it is today. . . . One of the nicest things Joe did for me when I was a youngster was to give me a beat-up old cornet of his which he had blown

JEREMY JAMES
To
ELEANOR LAMBERT

Above, screen depicting Audrey Pleydell-Bouverie.

for years. I prized that horn and guarded it with my life. I blew on it for a long, long time before I was fortunate enough to get another one."

When Sheldon Tannen was just beginning his apprenticeship at New York's 21 Club, his uncle, Mac Kriendler, presented him with white gloves and a top hat. Tannen pointed out that he didn't even own a set of tails, in fact had no use for them. "You will," said his uncle—and he was right.

Show business, it has been noted, elevates appreciation to the status of love. On Broadway, as in Hollywood, emotions run high. A word of praise at the right time, a token of tribute in the right place, is what keeps the whole fragile ark of talent and striving afloat, what makes it possible for the show to go on. Once Hedda Hopper, the powerful society reporter of the thirties, whom Hollywood both courted and dreaded, blasted Joan Fontaine in her column. Joan Bennett countered in defense of her friend with a live skunk delivered in a hatbox to the columnist's door.

It was great admiration that Cecil B. de Mille and the cast of *Joan the Woman* expressed to Geraldine Farrar, the temperamental diva who had nonetheless submitted to ordeals beyond the call of stardom. To authenticate her portrayal of France's heroine, she was dragged from her horse, immersed in burning oil, and literally set alight at the stake, protected from incineration by a coating of a solution that left her "only slightly singed." Judging such dedication to be deserving of more than a cast party, Farrar's colleagues presented her with a heavy silver mirror inscribed with their names and embossed on its handle with a bas-relief of Joan of Arc.

When teamwork achieves the desired result, a toast of champagne is adequate thanks. But when collaboration has been the key to unprecedented success, more exuberant measures are called for. Duke Ellington's largesse to his band was proverbial. One Christmas he called them together a week before the holiday. "Look, fellas," he said, "this has been a good year, a very good year all around. This is a very Merry Christmas for me, and I sincerely hope it will be for you. I got something for you, don't know whether it suits everybody's taste; after all some people like different colors, different models. But maybe you'll like this stuff," and to each one in turn—Barney, "Cootie," Rabbit, Tricky, Tizol, Freddy Guy—he parceled out a package. The wrappings were in every color, but the contents all were green. Duke knew his men needed cash to bring Christmas to their families, so he handed it out in the most graceful way he could think of.

Barron Hilton's style was somewhat flashier. The hotel magnate's love of sellout performances at his Las Vegas Hilton and Liberace's passion for rings on every finger coincided on the pianist's thirtieth anniversary show, when Hilton spotlighted their multimillion dollar contract with a *tour de force* of a ring shaped like a Steinway and made out of diamonds with a keyboard of ivory and onyx.

When *Shirley MacLaine on Broadway* broke house records at the Gershwin Theater, the show's producers felt that an outsize thank-you to their star was in order. MacLaine, who had done everything else in her brilliant career, once said she regretted never having ridden an elephant. On her fiftieth birthday, Ringling Brothers' prize pachyderm showed up at the theater and took the star on a stroll that backed traffic up to the Hudson.

In a reversal of the outflow of appreciation, the grateful star reaches out to thank all who made success possible. Gertrude Lawrence, flushed with her triumph in *The King and I*, presented the show's creators with exquisitely carved ivories of the children in the cast. Al Jolson gave producer Joseph Schenck a limousine decorated with tortoiseshell, engraved glass, and inlaid woodwork, which had won a design award at a Paris exhibition. Travis Banton, Hollywood's designer to the stars, received endless tributes: emerald cuff links from Marlene Dietrich, a champion dachshund from Kay Francis, a Dufy from Carole Lombard.

Barbra Streisand had some difficulty in locating just the right gift to express her appreciation to Vincente Minnelli for his fine direction of *On a Clear Day You Can See Forever*. She had decided that an unusual tea set would be the most appropriate. It had to be truly unusual, as Minnelli doesn't drink tea, but with persistence she found it—a tea set without a teapot. Across the creamer, she had engraved, "For the Cream of the Crop: For Vincente, Whom I Adore, Love Barbra, May 1969."

The network of support in show business is like groundcover in a forest, protecting the seedlings of striving from the harsh winds of self-doubt and the blight of cruel critics. Gifts between colleagues become talismans, symbols of enduring support and affection. Such were the pillows Mary Martin would needlepoint for her colleagues, and the ring depicting clasped hands that Richard Rodgers once gave her, starting a tradition between them that spilled over to their friends.

BARRON HILTON To LIBERACE

Above, Liberace's rings.

Above, Mary Martin and friends.
Pillows made by Mary Martin.

Talismans, too, were the ritual exchanges of clothing among performers. Sammy Davis Jr. prizes above gold the jackets deeded to him by Marlon Brando and James Dean, and the Stetson that John Wayne wore in *Stagecoach* and passed on to Davis with the tribute: "I didn't even let the kids touch this hat, it was very dear to me. But I guess you'll be able to find a home for it."

Although the hard world of commerce would seem impervious to comparable gestures of esteem, yet even in the anatomy of the politician and the capitalist there can beat a grateful heart. When J.P. Morgan successfully negotiated a delicate transfer of Central's stock, a grateful Cornelius Vanderbilt thanked his colleague with a costly silver service commissioned from Tiffany, instructing that the dies be destroyed to prevent duplication.

Even the corporation, that most dehumanized agent of capitalism, has proved an ardent gift giver when pleased with one of its own. Well aware that their famous child actress, Elizabeth Taylor, had fallen in love with her co-star in *National Velvet*, the equine equivalent of Prince Charles, Metro-Goldwyn-Mayer gave her the valuable steed—lock, stock, and saddle.

To mark the seventy-fifth birthday of their chairman, David Sarnoff, RCA presented the dedicated smoker with an eighteen-carat-gold thermidor in the shape of a book, its spine and the RCA emblem on its cover encrusted in diamonds.

Aspiring to the practical, Capitol Records offered to install in violinist Nathan Milstein's Fifth Avenue apartment state-of-the-art stereophonic equipment. For days workmen hammered and plastered, until at last the ultimate in sound technology was in place. At the inaugural moment, the corporation's president was on hand, champagne at the ready. However, there was a slight problem: the eminent musician did not own a record. The following day, Capitol dispatched ten cartons of classical hits, but as no shelves had been provided, they were relegated to the basement for permanent retirement.

This fiasco was mild in comparison with RCA's gift to Cole Porter. In a parallel effort, they offered to install in the composer's Waldorf Tower apartment the most advanced high-fidelity equipment, components that would not be available to the public for several years. "Terrific," said Cole, "please consult with my decorator," and left for California. Billy Baldwin was less enchanted, having lined the living room with fifteenth-century Venetian glass, crystal sconces, and irreplaceable bibelots. However, accommodation was made, and when Cole returned, RCA's executives were there to greet him with the inevitable champagne. "Would you like to turn on the system?" they asked, and Cole pushed the button. There was an explosion of glass as the panels crashed and the sconces splintered and the bibelots crashed to the ground. "The only things that didn't end up on the floor," Cole observed, "were the RCA executives, who were frozen in horror." Cole switched off the system and said, "I thank you very much for your generous gift and please don't ask me to name that tune." It was never turned on again, though RCA swore it had been adjusted. "I am not going to find out because I am afraid this button is really the doomsday button and if I press it again it is the end of the earth." The mirrors were never replaced, but neither was the system removed. "It was a magnificent gift after all; if only it had been reserved for my retirement," lamented the aesthete, who understandably would have liked a few more years to enjoy his unmarred reflection.

Retirement, of course, commands the last hurrah of tribute, the hip hip hooray of a lifetime well dedicated. In 1854, when Commodore William K. Garrison retired as mayor, the citizens of San Francisco presented him with a solid-gold tea service weighing forty-two pounds, said to be the only one in America at that time, preceding those of Mrs. Astor and Mrs. Vanderbilt by thirty years. When the Commodore later married, he presented his bride with the glittering service and proceeded with them both to New York, where the couple gained prompt entrée by hosting dazzling teas.

Those were flashy times, of course, and gold in our day weighs in a little more heavily, but Americans still like to say farewell with feeling and fanfare. Let the more recent retirement of one Judge Richard Comerford, district court justice of Leominster, Massachusetts, reflect the mind-set of the nation. Deciding that a gold watch would be insufficient tribute for Comerford's two decades of service to the community, his colleagues commissioned craftsmen to carve a grandfather clock and to etch on its glass door the Judge's portrait and a dedication. So difficult proved the task that the glass shattered twice, but the order stood until ultimately it was achieved. If their beloved Judge could devote twenty years to forestalling wrong, the least he deserved, his colleagues felt, was three costly tries at getting their expression of gratitude right.

His Crew
To William F. Buckley, Jr.

William F. Buckley, Jr., best-selling author, commentator, and host of television's *Firing Line*, is as intrepid a sailor as he is a conservative. In 1980, he set out from the Caribbean island of St. Thomas with four friends, four professional crew members, and photographer Christopher Little on a voyage that would be documented in Buckley and Little's book, *Atlantic High*.

They sailed through the Bahamas and the Azores, pulling in to Marbella thirty sea-tossed days later.

The crew marked their enthusiasm for the adventure by giving Buckley this piece of scrimshaw, which shows a detailed map of the entire journey.

Above, William F. Buckley, Jr.

AIMÉ MAEGHT
To
STANLEY MARCUS

When distinguished French art dealer Aimé Maeght visited Texas, Stanley Marcus, Chairman Emeritus of Neiman-Marcus Company, was honored to give a dinner party for him. Maeght seemed especially pleased with the simple American fare his host chose for the evening, as well as with the superlative wine and the cultivated company.

After dinner, Marcus showed the art dealer his miniature books. Maeght was delighted with the extensive collection. He invited Marcus to visit him on his next trip to France, and promised that he would show him his only miniature book, which had the unusual feature of including an original drawing by Joan Miró.

A few months later, Maeght returned Marcus's hospitality by giving an elegant luncheon in Paris. Wondering how the final course could compete with the culinary delights he had already sampled, Marcus waited expectantly for the dome to be lifted from his dessert plate.

There, instead of a confection, Marcus found the Miró book—a much greater treat than he could ever have imagined.

Above, Stanley Marcus.

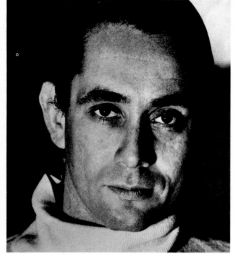

JACQUES KUGEL
To
KENNETH JAY LANE

Above right, Kenneth Jay Lane.

Shortly after his marriage, jewelry designer Kenny Lane was in Paris with his wife and visited art dealer Jacques Kugel. Lane admired a charming painting by artist Ferdinand Wachsmuth. "Do you really like it? Could you really live with it?" Kugel asked. Lane responded positively. "Then I want you to have it as a wedding present." Lane was surprised, since it was a valuable painting.

Then Lane noticed the pair of columns, one lapis, one malachite, he had sold Kugel years earlier. "Wait," said Kugel, and he showed Lane how the columns worked. It turned out that they were royal games and much more valuable than Lane had known.

Kugel's gift then became clear. "It is a gift of justice, which proves that Kugel is the best *antiquaire* in the world, with the most discerning eye," says Lane.

112

This gift of a gold-and-crystal clock, with its intricate mechanism that rotates to indicate simultaneously time zones throughout the world, symbolizes the delicate relationship between patient and doctor.

Sayyid Hamad Bin Hamoud, Minister of Diwan Affairs in the Sultanate of Oman, went to the Texas Heart Institute in August 1983, expecting to have a heart bypass operation. But after an extensive evaluation of the patient's symptoms, renowned heart surgeon Dr. Denton Cooley decided that his condition could be managed with medical treatment, making the delicate operation unnecessary.

This clock, which was to have expressed His Excellency's thanks for a skillful operation, was instead presented to the surgeon in gratitude for his sound diagnosis and considerate handling of the case.

Dr. Cooley says, "I was impressed that he would be so generous, as it seemed to me that my services were modest by comparison."

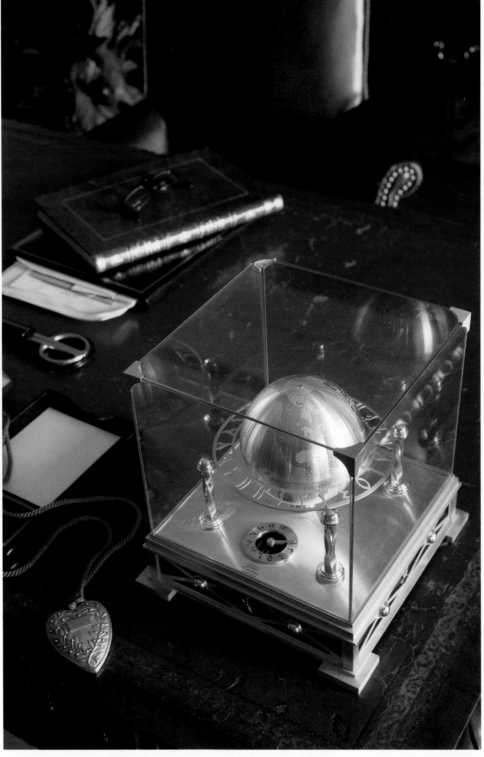

Above, Dr. Denton Cooley.

"You really know how to do it and you did it," read the note folded into a little silver matchbox that arrived backstage for Gwen Verdon on the opening night of Cole Porter's *Can-Can* in May of 1953. Tucked under the note was a pair of antique jet earrings.

The earrings were a gift from a longtime friend and dance partner, the great jazz dancer Jack Cole, whose arresting performances "shocked the viewers with their voltage" and whose revolutionary inventiveness was key to the development of America's musical theater.

Hollywood's loss was Broadway's gain when Jack Cole brought his choreographic fireworks to such hits as *Kismet, A Funny Thing Happened on the Way to the Forum,* and *Man of La Mancha.*

Broadway gained another star that night when Verdon electrified audience, critics, and Jack Cole alike with her sizzling dance numbers. From the minor role of Claudine in 892 performances of *Can-Can,* she went on to star in *Damn Yankees* and to revel in a long Broadway career that included husband Bob Fosse's shows *Sweet Charity* and *Chicago.*

It all began for her that opening night of *Can-Can.* So meaningful was Cole's tribute that the earrings became Gwen Verdon's signature piece: "I wore them in every single show I've

ever done. I wore them in *Damn Yankees;* they are on the cover of *Time* and the cover of *Life.* I treasure the note even more, but you can't go around wearing a note."

Above, Gwen Verdon and Jack Cole.

PABLO PICASSO
To
JOHN RICHARDSON

John Richardson: "As an art historian, I have had more than my share of presents from artists—Picasso in particular. This incomparably generous man once made me a cut-out paper tie when I was unexpectedly invited to a smart reception ('They'll never let you in without one') and a paper crown for an even dressier affair."

In the 1950s, Richardson lived in Provence, where he and collector Douglas Cooper had restored an old chateau and filled it with a great collection of Cubist art. Picasso and his wife Jacqueline would often join them, an entourage in tow, to attend the local bullfights.

"One day, in connection with a book I was writing, I showed Picasso a photograph of a fake drawing I had spotted in one of Sotheby's catalogues. Would he be so good as to denounce it so that some half-witted collector would not be fooled? I asked. A few days later, he mailed the photograph back to me with the word *faux* (fake) scrawled across it and the false signature crossed out. On the back, he had executed this handsome ink-wash drawing of a bullfight, duly inscribed to me.

" 'You see, I've developed a secret process,' he joked when I thanked him. 'It transforms photographs of fakes into authentic Picassos. But don't tell Sotheby's!' "

Above, the fake Picasso.

Above, Morton Gottlieb and Dasha Epstein.

Broadway producers Dasha Epstein and Morton Gottlieb are old friends as well as close colleagues. On the occasion of his success with *Same Time Next Year,* which opened on March 13, 1975, Gottlieb showed his appreciation of his colleague by giving her billing as one of the producers of the play.

Epstein, in turn, expressed her admiration for Gottlieb by presenting him for one of his birthdays with a carefully drawn replica of the show's publicity poster, which depicted the eight successive stars of the two-character play in bed. The replica was exact but for one important detail. In place of each of the leading men disporting himself in turn with Ellen Burstyn, Joyce Van Patten, Loretta Swit, and Sandy Dennis, Epstein had substituted Morton Gottlieb. What better gift than to share such "intimacy" with four wonderful leading ladies?

Actress Greer Garson, wise in the ways of the theater, film, and television, speaks from experience and with deep feeling about a particular gift on a special occasion: "'What would you like best for our thirtieth wedding anniversary?' my husband asked me. Now Buddy (Colonel E.E. Fogelson) is infinitely resourceful in such matters, having delighted me through the years with such unexpected gifts as a mountain in New Mexico, a baby elephant in California, an island in the river Pecos, a party graced by a quartet of symphony first-chair violinists, and a prize white shorthorn bull and seven snowy heifers brought from Scotland.

"But the best gift of all was neither material nor tangible, although very visible in its ongoing effects. For our thirtieth anniversary, he endowed in my name some annual awards for drama students at Southern Methodist University in Dallas. Remembering my own early days and how hard it was to get started in the performing arts, I am happy to think we are giving a little help to eager beginners at a difficult time. Other gifts are temporary pleasures or warm memories, but this gift lives and progresses each year.

"In trying to pictorialize the awards to drama students, we used the beautiful wooden masks which were in their own right a treasured gift, carved for me by Brother Joseph Miller at The College of Santa Fe, to celebrate the seventeenth anniversary of the Greer Garson Theatre Center on campus. The royal robe and crown were used in a student production of *Pippin*. The books were borrowed from the Fogelson Library Center, also on campus. As you see, we are both happily involved with Academe and the Muses."

"LOOK NOT FOR REWARD FROM OTHERS
BUT HOPE THAT YOU HAVE DONE YOUR BEST"

Remark of Winston Churchill to Walter H. Annenberg on the occasion of a stag dinner given in
Sir Winston's honor by Bernard Baruch March 20, 1949, Sherry's, Park Avenue, New York City

WINSTON CHURCHILL *To* WALTER ANNENBERG

Walter Annenberg could not have foreseen his ambassadorship to the Court of St. James when he found himself seated next to Sir Winston Churchill at a New York stag dinner party given by Bernard Baruch in 1949. He was delighted and somewhat awed: "After all, he was the greatest leader of our time." Nevertheless, he plucked up his courage: "About one in the morning, after endless wines and beakers of brandy, I turned to Churchill and said, 'Sir, I hope you don't think me presumptuous, but I must tell you how saddened I was at the electorate in your country rejecting you as they did after you had saved their empire and their way of life.' Now he could have shriveled me up with a few well-chosen words, but he looked at me for about ten seconds, put his hand on my shoulder, and said, 'Young Annenberg, look not for rewards from others but hope you have done your best.' After about ten minutes of very privileged conversation, he said, 'Annenberg, I am going to do something I rarely do, which is to leave my autographed picture for you upon my departure. Don't tell anyone until I am out of the country because I don't readily hand out my autograph to people!' "

In the following years, Annenberg became a collector of the rare, but the place of honor is reserved for this autographed portrait, taken in 1941 by Yousuf Karsh, "probably as fine a gift as I have ever received."

Above, Jimmy Carter and Robert Strauss.

JIMMY CARTER
To
ROBERT STRAUSS

Following his defeat for reelection, President Jimmy Carter gave his campaign chairman, Robert Strauss, this Norman Rockwell print of a sleek campaign manager walking out on a wiped-out candidate.

Carter inscribed the print, "To my good friend and Campaign Chairman Bob Strauss, thanks for making it all possible," and presented the framed tribute to him at the White House while two hundred people looked on—proving that you can't keep a good sense of humor down.

WILLIAM PALEY AND EDWARD R. MURROW *To* DANNY KAYE

When UNICEF was still the poor relation of the United Nations, Danny Kaye volunteered to raise funds for their most urgent health programs by making a television documentary for CBS's *See It Now*. In the course of filming it, Kaye visited UNICEF installations all over the world, singing and dancing with children in malaria centers and in leper colonies, donating his time and his talent to underscoring their plight.

The Secret Life of Danny Kaye proved to be an unprecedented triumph. It was shown simultaneously all over the world. It was more than a television show: its reception was fraught with emotion and helped launch UNICEF as one of the greatest health organizations in the world.

To express their appreciation for the outstanding contribution of this great humanitarian, CBS's William Paley and *See It Now*'s Edward R. Murrow commissioned from the artist David Stone Martin this rendering of the comedian as Gulliver, engulfed by all the children of the world. This image was given official standing subsequently when Kaye was named Ambassador to the Children of the World and accorded a diplomatic passport under that title, which he still holds.

Alma Spreckels is remembered as one of early California's most colorful personalities. She channeled her husband's large sugar fortune into bringing artists and art to San Francisco.

One of her more remarkable endeavors was inspired by a temporary pavilion that had been erected to represent France at San Francisco's Panama-Pacific International Exposition of 1915. Alma convinced her husband of the need for a more permanent memorial—an art museum, the California Palace of the Legion of Honor, which would be dedicated to the Californian soldiers who died in World War I and would stand as a symbol of the friendship between France and America.

Among those who responded to Alma Spreckels' efforts was Victoria Melita, Grand Duchess of Russia, who donated this magnificent tea service as a gift to her, accompanied by the following letter:

Cannes, 11th February 1922

Dear Mrs. Spreckels—

Having heard of your wonderful new museum, and of all you are doing to help my sister the Queen of Roumania, I wish to present you with a golden tea service made by our famous Russian artist Fabergé. It is one of our few treasures saved and I am glad if it can find a place in the glorious monument you are building to the memory of your California soldiers. It has always been a tradition in the Russian Imperial family to help whenever they could, however they could, and wherever they could, and as at this moment we cannot build anything in remembrance of our own millions of fallen brave, who fought and fell for the same cause, I am happy to offer a token of respect and regard to your 3,600 California sons whom you are immortalizing.

Yours very sincerely,
Victoria Melita Grand Duchess Kirill of Russia

GRAND DUCHESS KIRILL OF RUSSIA
To
ALMA DE BRETTEVILLE SPRECKELS

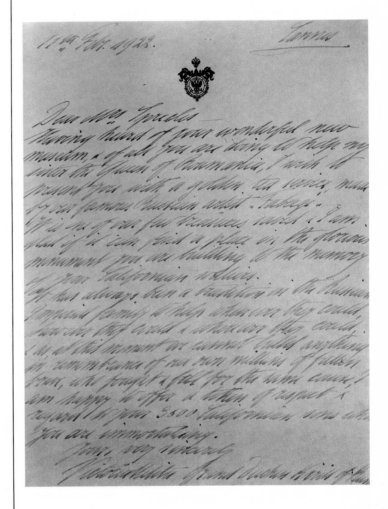

Above, letter from the Grand Duchess.

ABBA SCHWARTZ
To
ARTHUR SCHLESINGER, JR.

Above right, Arthur Schlesinger, Jr.

In 1982, historian and author Arthur Schlesinger, Jr., was appointed chairman of New York State's observance of the hundredth birthday of Franklin D. Roosevelt. Schlesinger, who has written *The Age of Roosevelt,* was happy to serve and to renew his contacts with many individuals whose lives have been affected by the Roosevelt legacy.

One was Abba Schwartz, a close friend of Eleanor Roosevelt's. As thanks for his work on the centennial, Schwartz presented Schlesinger with this reproduction of a private printing, signed by Roosevelt, of FDR's first inaugural address (in which is found: "The only thing we have to fear is fear itself."). Schlesinger says, "I treasure this because the address changed American history—and here it is in a beautiful edition inscribed by FDR himself."

Léon Blum was France's first Jewish and first Socialist premier, the great leader of the Popular Front in the years before World War II. In 1940, the Vichy government arrested him on charges of war guilt and imprisoned him until the end of the war.

Blum, his health much impaired, was freed by the U.S. forces. In 1950, America's new Ambassador to France, David Bruce, and his wife, Evangeline, paid Blum a visit and found him in very poor condition. As they were leaving, Blum told Mrs. Bruce that he would like to give her something that had meant a great deal to him. "He handed me a battered little metal cup. 'This,' he said, 'was the only object I had with me throughout my imprisonment.' A few months later, he died. It is rather touching."

Above, Evangeline Bruce and daughter Alexandra in Paris.

IRA GERSHWIN *To* VINCENTE MINNELLI

One Christmas, lyricist Ira Gershwin turned up at the home of Vincente Minnelli with an unusual gift. It was a large watercolor, a self-portrait of his brother, George Gershwin, that had rarely been seen.

Ira knew the painting would be meaningful to Minnelli: the renowned director of *Meet Me in Saint Louis* and the celebrated composer of *Rhapsody in Blue* had worked and played together after the Gershwin brothers moved to Hollywood.

Years later, Ira and Vincente collaborated on the film *An American in Paris*—inspired by George's symphonic poem—which won an Oscar in 1951. So Ira passed the portrait along to his friend—their friend—with the warm dedication: "Self-portrait of the composer of *An American in Paris*, George Gershwin, for my good friend Vincente Minnelli, its director, from Ira Gershwin, its lyric writer and friend and admirer of Vincente Minnelli. Christmas 1951."

SIR JOHN GIELGUD
To ROBERT FIZDALE AND ARTHUR GOLD

Noted concert duo-pianists Arthur Gold and Robert Fizdale embarked on a second brilliant career when they wrote *Misia*, the much-acclaimed biography of Misia Sert. Now they are preparing a biography of the legendary actress Sarah Bernhardt.

Robert Fizdale: "We did a great deal of research in France, then went to London and saw our old friend John Gielgud, who came and spent four hours with us talking about Sarah Bernhardt. He knew her very well because he was the son of the actress Kate Terry and the nephew of Ellen Terry, who was the most famous English actress of the time and Sarah Bernhardt's close friend in England.

"From the time Gielgud was five years old, he was taken to all Sarah's performances. He was nineteen when she died, but by that time he was already an actor, so he had observed her with great interest and collected all sorts of memorabilia. Thus he was able to tell us a great deal about her. He then gave us this wonderful

poster of Bernhardt, created around 1890 by Mucha, the great Czechoslovakian artist who did all of Bernhardt's early posters. The smaller versions of these posters are not as well known and are much richer in color; this one brought us, after a long year of research, fresh inspiration and great pleasure. We feel Gielgud is the greatest actor of his time, just as Bernhardt was the greatest actress of her time."

Above, Arthur Gold and Robert Fizdale.

131

Vincent Price: "It would have been around the end of the war. Max Beckmann, Germany's great Expressionist painter, had sought refuge in the States and was teaching here. One day my friend Morton D. May (of the May Company), who had an extensive collection of Beckmann's work, called to tell me that the artist would be visiting Los Angeles and asked if I would gather some people to meet him.

"Well, I hustled everybody I could—Billy Brice, Howard Warshaw, all the painters who were friends of mine. Beckmann's wonderful wife, Quappi (the model for many of his paintings), translated for those who didn't speak German. It was a very jolly afternoon.

"As he left, Beckmann said, 'I would like to send you a drawing.' Soon afterward, he died. I wrote Quappi a letter of condolence, because although I really didn't know them, I felt very close to them.

"I had completely forgotten about his promise, but about six months later a package arrived, and it was this drawing with a note from Quappi that said: 'Max had picked this out to send you, and I was having a terrible time going through his estate, and I found this and wanted to send it to you as Max's wish.' The drawing depicts cabaret scenes, which were typical of that period of German Expressionism."

Above, reverse of Beckmann drawing.

133

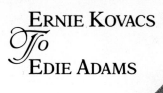

ERNIE KOVACS
To
EDIE ADAMS

Edie Adams: "Ernie was always giving unusual gifts and he never did anything in moderation. Where everyone else had a charm bracelet, he gave me so many charms, I had them made into a charm belt. A lot of the charms have to do with cooking and the kitchen. It was an on-going joke that started with this gold sink, which he had made up with doors that swing open, and cleaning things inside, because he wanted me to recognize a kitchen sink if I ever saw one.

"Then there was a can opener, and then for our fifth anniversary a gold kitchen faucet with a diamond drop of water that said, 'Five cinca years, love and kisses.' That was Ernie. They don't make them like that any more."

THE

Humorous

GIFT

Were you to ask Bob Hope the meaning of *giving*, he might point out that it is a verb with interesting potential. One can, after all, give notice, offense, or fair warning. One can also give off, give way, give over, and give up. One can eventually give out. All this is to say that giving has a light side, an unalterably bright side, as is proved by the comedic efforts of some to put fun into their obligations.

Take Harry Blackstone, the classic illusionist. He thoughtfully surprised his wife on their anniversary with a diamond ring. He slipped it onto her finger with a warm embrace, a gesture she was quick to return. Not quick enough, however; when she looked back at her hand, the ring had disappeared.

Charlie Chaplin staged a more elaborate presentation to Oona. She had admired a ruby-and-diamond bracelet at a Beverly Hills jeweler's but thought the price excessive. Chaplin told the salesman they would think about it and steered Oona out of the store. As they reached their car, he became visibly nervous. "Drive on quickly," he urged, and with trembling fingers produced the loot. Oona paled and pulled over, pleading with him to return it. Chaplin confessed: he had applied his legendary sense of timing to buying the bracelet while his wife's attention was diverted.

The wits, of course, have an edge on mere mortals. Gags go flying back and forth between them in sundry forms, inert and alive. There was not a more dedicated gagster than comedian Ernie Kovacs. Once he and Jackie Gleason competed for months to see who could give the biggest bouquet. When they had worked their way up to racing garlands and could find nothing larger, they moved on to dead flowers. Kovacs lived down the hill from Frank Sinatra, which triggered the running gag of the portable john. Kovacs had positioned one for the workmen who were remodeling his house, and Sinatra started leaving corny messages in it each time he passed by. Finally, for Christmas, Kovacs bought Sinatra his very own portable john and had it dumped in his driveway.

Sometimes the ribber pays dearly for his fun. Saudi Arabian businessman Adnan Khashoggi started a tradition years ago of giving his devoted chief of staff, Bob Shaheen, the monetary equivalent of his age times a thousand when his birthday rolls around. As Shaheen has grown older, he has also gotten wiser; since Khashoggi must pay in the currency of the country the pair find themselves in on that date, Shaheen has devised some elaborate stratagems to land them in places where the exchange rate is in his favor. One year he talked the captain of Khashoggi's yacht into detouring the craft, sailing it from the Turkish coast into international waters. There they paused just long enough to stamp papers that would prove Shaheen's birthday had not been devaluated.

In the realm of the prank, none surpasses the one you ask for. When actress Carole Lombard moved into a house on Hollywood Boulevard, Billy Haines generously offered to donate his services as decorator, asking only that she showcase the result to Hollywood at a white-tie party. Lombard duly obliged, but was bitten by an urge she couldn't resist. On the big night, while Haines was at home changing into tails, Lombard had the furniture and rugs he had so carefully selected carted off and replaced with the trappings of a barnyard. When he arrived, he found Hollywood's finest dressed in overalls, chewing straw as they admired "his" decor. (Lombard gave a second reception for him, with the real decor, later.)

Animal exchanges have always been good for a laugh. When Cole Porter was living in Beverly Hills, one evening the doorbell rang. "Sign here," the houseman was told as he was left holding a rope. On the other end was a six-month-old elephant. A card attached read: "This trunk call says it all. To Coley from Noley." Refusing to be outdone, Cole retorted in kind, depositing a live alligator on Noel Coward's front doorstep with the message "Here are some teeth to match your tongue. To Noley from Coley."

"What darn fool would buy one of those?" exclaimed her mother, Mrs. Ralph Lowe, to Houston oil magnate Mary Ralph Lowe Yost. They were watching television news coverage of Neiman-Marcus's 1967 feature Christmas offering, His and Her Camels. On Christmas Day Mrs. Lowe's doorbell rang and in walked a baby camel. The gift card suspended around its neck read, "Merry Christmas, from your daughter the darn fool."

Paul Newman had just moved into an apartment in New York that was perfect except that, as he complained to Robert Redford, his balcony was overrun with pigeons. A short time later he received a housewarming present from his friend—two crates full of pigeons.

It was in a somewhat larger crate that the swashbuckling Errol Flynn received his most memorable tribute. Among his avid fans, the most persistent

MARY RALPH LOWE YOST
To
ERMA LOWE

Above, Erma the camel.

George Marshall
To
Winston Churchill

Above, Winston Churchill and his globe.

had been a girl from the Midwest. She would write to him weekly with assurances of her devotion and, incidentally, of a present that would be arriving. It was to come by special delivery on a specified Saturday. Flynn was sufficiently intrigued to be hanging around when the truck pulled through the gate with a crate that it took two men to unload. Flynn called in some friends and, convinced that they had heard strange noises inside, they warily pried off the top. Out popped his fan, very attractive, as everyone recalled, and wearing a bathing suit. Flynn was so amused that he placed a call to her friends back home, confirming her coup. "This is Errol Flynn in Hollywood," he said. "Your girlfriend is sitting here with me having a drink and enjoying the view." Drinks lasted four days, after which his present of a lifetime went home.

Winston Churchill, who enjoyed a good joke as much as a good cigar, once quipped that he could never figure out the South Pole, since he was not able to stand on his head. His good friend General George Marshall therefore had a globe built on ball bearings so that the warlord could easily turn it upside down and study the South Pole with ease. Churchill's thanks came back promptly in the form of a photograph of himself pointing triumphantly north to the great southern ice floe.

Another arch ribber, Art Buchwald, recalls that his most successful inspiration was his gift to Robert and Ethel Kennedy on the occasion of their seventeenth wedding anniversary. "They were having a big outdoor blowout at Hickory Hill, so I went to an insurance broker and bought them rain insurance for the evening. If it rained one quarter of an inch, then they would get fifteen thousand dollars. I had it framed in case it didn't rain (which it didn't!) so they could keep the policy forever."

One Christmas, Buchwald's daughter, Jennifer, turned the tables on him. Tired of hearing her father introduce himself on the lecture circuit as a high school dropout, she appealed to his Forest Hills alma mater. With the approval of New York's Board of Education, they issued a belated diploma on the grounds of the subject's proven literacy. Buchwald says he was delighted, "though it ruined my whole speech. I still say I have no diploma, but now I am lying."

Christmas was also the occasion of the classic calendar gag. For years, Henry Pearlstone, of the Dallas insurance firm Pearlstone and Elliott, sent calendars to his clients. "Henry," they would protest, "please stop it with those calendars"—but the calendars kept right on coming. Then one Christmas season an inordinate number of presents began arriving at the Pearlstones'. There were scarf boxes, jewelry boxes, suit boxes. It was all Pearlstone could talk about; the twenty-fifth couldn't arrive fast enough. Christmas morning, he rushed down to open them and out of each package, the large and the small, emerged a calendar—German calendars, Jewish calendars, rolled and folding and spiral-bound calendars. His friends Robert Strauss and Jack Goldstein had conspired to pull them in from all over the world. It was, needless to say, the last time Henry Pearlstone sent out calendars for Christmas.

For sheer effrontery, none has bested Fred Higgenstonough. One Friday in the forties, the wealthy playboy walked into Bergdorf Goodman's fur department with a beautiful blonde on his arm and asked to see a mink coat. He selected the most expensive one. "I'll take it," he said. "Here's my check. Put her initials in the lining and we'll call for it next Tuesday." When he returned, he was summoned to an embarrassed credit manager, whose duty it was to inform Higgenstonough that his check had not cleared. Fred only smiled. "Good," he said, "and thanks for a very pleasant weekend."

Between spouses, such antics could be grounds for divorce, unless one's partner had a good sense of humor. Richard Aldrich had a pair of gold handcuffs made for his beloved wife, actress Gertrude Lawrence. The connotation was: "Let's see if you can get out of this, Lady Houdini." They were ungainly and massive, cast as they were from the real thing, but Gertie adored them and sported them often, albeit both on one wrist.

The joke that collector Stanley Marsh devised for his wife, Wendy, was somewhat larger in scale. Irked by the continual debating of the question "What is art?" one year for her birthday Marsh decided to give his wife exactly that, A R T. He crafted the three letters into giant versions of the sort of alphabet blocks children play with. Each was eight feet tall and six feet wide, and they were painted, respectively, primary red, yellow, and blue. "So now," beams Marsh, "if anybody wants to know what art is, it is three letters leaning against the fence in the backyard of our house, Toad Hall, in Amarillo, Texas."

It was a long time before young working actors Margo and Eddie Albert could take a meaningful vacation. They consulted on where to go, but it soon became obvious that Margo's dream of the Greek islands was fading before Eddie's plans for a fishing trip to Baja. Margo's gloom deepened as pamphlets on marlin and Mexican hotels began piling up. Finally, one day a large packet arrived with their tickets. It was the last straw. Margo was disgusted: "The last time I had caught a mahi-mahi it was like killing a rainbow. I had dreamt of Greece, the proportions, the light. 'It's too late now,' Eddie said, 'here are the tickets and we're going fishing.' He opened the packet and tossed it to me. And out spilled Delos and Mykonos and our own boat and crew for three weeks in the islands. This incredible gift spread out at my feet, like a dream."

William du Pont Carpenter didn't just want a birthday surprise for his wife, an attractive woman who closely resembled (and always dressed in the style of) actress Hedy Lamarr; he wanted to stage a scenario she would never forget. He arranged a dinner party predating her birthday by some weeks. On the home front, he forewarned his wife that he could not see his way to buying her the emerald she had admired at Harry Winston's but would try to find something else she would like. When Frances Carpenter appeared at what she had thought was to be a small family dinner, there were all her women friends costumed exactly as she was, with Hedy Lamarr wigs and black dresses dripping in rhinestones. "I thought I would die. I had never seen anything so funny." Then, after dinner, the children brought in all the presents. "I opened them in turn—silly, fun things. In my son's box was some rumpled paper and a pretty green stone. I gave him a hug and went on to the next box. 'Frances,' said my best friend, 'you'd better look at that again.' She was hysterical. In fact, everyone looked horrified. They knew, of course, that the box held the fabulous Winston emerald and thought I was about to toss it out with the tissue paper."

Packaging is the framework for the perennial joke gift, the temptingly large parcel that promises the world—until you work your way through graduated boxes to end with a prize the size of a pea. It was fitting that Christo, the maverick artist who has wrapped works and phenomena from the Chicago Art Museum to the oceanfront at Newport, should have devised the ultimate gift-packaging gag. He had an enormous package delivered to friends. They excavated eagerly through dense layers of wrapping to find nothing but a card at the center. It read, "Congratulations, you have just destroyed an original Christo."

EDWARD BOREIN
To WILL ROGERS

In the late 1920s, humorist Will Rogers enjoyed sitting in his easy chair at his California home and lassoing his guests—a routine that did not always amuse his nearest and dearest.

One friend and frequent visitor, Western cowboy artist Edward Borein, grew impatient with being roped every time he entered the room, so after one of his visits, he sent this stuffed calf, with a note: "Here, Will, rope this for a change, and save the wear and tear on your family and friends."

The calf was obviously well received, as is evidenced by the loss of its ears. Will's children would drag it around the room while Will roped it—his way of relaxing.

Above, painting by Edward Borein.

Comedian Jack Benny, renowned for his thrift, made fun of his own parsimony by giving George Burns this money clip. Made of genuine gold (which stunned them both), it features a Bouché caricature of Burns on one side and one of Benny on the other.

Holding the ever-present cigar, George Burns notes: "Fifty years ago, I was thirty-eight. Jack was thirty-nine when I first met him. Jack was always thirty-nine, Jack stayed thirty-nine. Jack died when he was thirty-nine; he died a young man."

Burns further observes: "Here is the money clip. It was a great gift—and it had a dollar bill inserted in it. As he gave me the clip, Jack said 'I have a little bad news for you.' I asked if he wanted the clip back and Jack said, 'Heck no, I want the dollar bill back!'

"That was Jack Benny, the perennial thirty-nine-year-old tightwad. But the Jack Benny I knew was entirely different. He was really something special. He was the warmest and most considerate man I ever knew."

George has carried the money clip with him every day since he got it. The gift never leaves him. As George says, "Jack is gone and part of me went with him, but a lot of Jack stayed here with me."

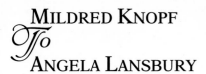

MILDRED KNOPF
To
ANGELA LANSBURY

Cookbook author Mildred Knopf: "When my friend Angela Lansbury announced that she was going to buy or build a house, I wondered how I could contribute something to enhance her new home and at the same time express my personal devotion. Brilliant actress as she is, it occurred to me that her outstanding characteristic, perhaps less well known, is her dedication to her husband and her children. I decided to express in a tapestry this remarkable side of her character.

"Each floral square represents a letter of the alphabet, for instance, the first letter of Angela's name is spelled with a tapestry picture of *A*nemones, followed, in turn, by *N*asturtium, *G*ladiola, and so on. I had her children, Anthony, Deirdre, and David, and her husband, Peter, follow in the same way. The family name of Shaw is whittled out of the trunk of the tree."

THE GIFT OF

Friendship

That Americans hold friendship in high regard is evidenced by the extent of gift giving among friends. Virtually every date marked in red on the calendar serves as an occasion for an exchange of presents that, be they serious or silly, are always appropriate and infallibly thoughtful, intentioned as they are to deepen the friendship they confirm.

Gift giving among friends has ranged in time and effort and expense from a flower to Fabergé, from the simplest greeting card to hail a significant event to the elaborate orchestration of the event itself. But whether it is as modest as a card or as costly as a Cadillac, the meaning conveyed has always been the same: You are my friend and I care for you.

Encouraged by merchandising but arising from a native expansiveness, the manner and motives of giving among friends reveal much about the American character. A group of Harvard undergraduates, aware that their talented friend Bernard Berenson could not afford to continue his education abroad, scraped together $750 to send him on that first voyage to Italy—a trip that was to have momentous repercussions in the course of art history.

In the same spirit, when President Wilson retired from the White House with no other house to go to (his distinguished background as a minister's son and academician having left him little personal wealth), a group of friends contributed ten thousand dollars each to provide him with a comfortable dwelling.

Cissy Patterson, the formidable editor of the *Washington Herald,* found a way to reciprocate the continual generosity of her friend Marion Davies. She coaxed Miss Davies down from San Simeon on the pretext of needing advice on a present for her daughter and waited for her selection—an aquamarine-and-diamond necklace. She then had it wrapped and presented it to Davies on the spot, saying, "This was the only way I knew to find you something you wanted."

To express his lifelong devotion to Joseph and Caroline Choate, financier J.P. Morgan commemorated their fiftieth wedding anniversary with a token befitting the world's foremost collector of the rare and the costly: an opulently embossed 22-carat-gold caudle cup with salver.

The propensity for sharing motivated Helen Gould to divert her twenty-two gardeners from the upkeep of her 500-acre estate to the cultivation of thousands of hothouse orchids, with which she gifted her friends at Christmas.

The inclination to panache prompted eminent Hollywood producer Ray Stark to welcome his equally eminent colleague Aaron Spelling, to Spelling's new ten-million-dollar abode not with a traditional pot of azaleas or even a sapling, but with a full-grown redwood tree.

Tenderness moved Liza Minnelli to commemorate the many wonderful times she and her mother, Judy Garland, had shared with Sammy Davis Jr. by giving him a pair of Judy's dancing shoes.

Agent-producer Charlie Feldman developed thoughtfulness into a lifetime of generosity, distributing tokens like the Bentley that his lawyer Don Petroni still drives around Beverly Hills. He reached out to his friends even after his death by deeding them his artworks, each piece hand-delivered with its taxes prepaid: a Renoir to Billy Wilder, a Bernard Buffet to Louis Jourdan, and so on, to seventy-one people who had meant much to him during his lifetime.

Such a scattering of masterpieces might have ruined the dinner of old Joseph Duveen, purveyor of fine art to such as Henry Clay Frick and J.P. Morgan; he was known for tailoring the cost of an object to match the purse of a client. And yet even he came through royally for his friends. When banker Henry Goldman, a client of many lucrative years, became blind and unable to continue collecting, Duveen would stop in regularly to tell him the art gossip, and one Christmas he brought Goldman two Holbein miniatures, a gift he knew would give the old collector great pleasure even though he could not see them.

The gift to a friend is a bond, bridging differences, neutralizing contention. Despite their warm friendship, columnist Ann Landers and Vice President Hubert Humphrey were deeply divided about our nation's involvement in the Vietnam war. Humphrey assured her that if she spoke with General Westmoreland, she would understand why it was a war we should be in and a war we could win. Finally, Landers said she would go to Vietnam if she could also visit the men in the hospitals. Humphrey made the arrangements. When she returned to the States, still unconvinced, Humphrey handed her a small velvet box. "This is a peace offering," he said, "as well as a birthday gift." It was a gold vice-presidential seal, and the rubies and diamonds that circled it were embedded in an olive wreath.

One night when dining with Jackie and Bobby

J.P. Morgan
To
Joseph and Caroline Choate

Below, gold caudle cup and salver.

Above, Jourdan's Buffet painting.

Charlie Feldman
To
Louis Jourdan

Kennedy at the Plaza, Rudolf Nureyev and Leonard Bernstein fell to arguing over a musical point. "If I'm right," said Nureyev, "I'd like the emerald cross in the window of A La Vieille Russie." He was, but Bernstein understandably demurred, saying that the stake was a little high. A short time later, Bobby and Jackie Kennedy invited Nureyev to dinner at Orsini's, and there on his plate was a small package from A La Vieille Russie. Inside was a gold double-headed eagle set with emeralds and a note: "We are sorry it could not be the cross."

The gift to a friend is always appropriate, either to the occasion, as were the two copies of *Life Begins at Forty* that Frank Sinatra presented to Jack Benny on his eightieth birthday, or to the person himself, as were the blackamoor automata that cherished colleagues such as Jimmy Stewart and David Merrick kept adding to producer Josh Logan's collection. Merrick went the extra distance, as it happened, traveling to New Orleans for the opening of his friend's show *Kind Sir* so that he could present the gift in person backstage. "There he stood," recalls Logan warmly, "in the doorway, holding it in his hands."

Because the message of friendship is a personal one, the artist has a special edge on the means of conveying it. "I prefer to have something painted by a man than made by an oyster," said Louisine Havemayer, New York's great patron of the arts, who collected until she ran out of walls. The painter, the sculptor, the writer, are uniquely positioned to give of themselves.

When France's noted artist Fernand Léger had his first exhibition in the States, at New York's Museum of Modern Art, he told his close friends American painter Gerald Murphy and his wife, Sara, who had been instrumental in introducing him to the American art world, that there was one painting in the show he wanted them to have. Inviting them to look around, he told them that if they guessed which painting he had in mind, it was theirs. Sara found herself drawn to a work that was atypically muted, representing possibly a new direction for the artist. "Yes," said Léger, and turned the canvas over. On the back he had written: "Pour Sara et Gérald."

To express her affection for Pablo Picasso, America's doyenne of letters, Gertrude Stein, wrote one of her more surreal poems, detailing her vision of "something that had been coming out of him and it had meaning, a charming meaning, a solid meaning, a struggling meaning, a clear meaning." Stein

Above, Logan's automaton.

was somewhat cavalier about the reciprocal gift, however—Picasso's now noted portrait of her, for which she sat ninety-seven times—and wrote asking to exchange it for a painting of his she had recently seen and liked better. Vastly amused, Picasso showed her letter to painter Gerald Murphy, who was shocked and said so. "Yes," Picasso said, "but I love her so much!"

Two black-and-white etchings, one of an 8 and the other of an O were the medium that artist Jasper Johns chose to mark the eightieth birthday of his friend and patron Senator Jacob Javits. On the occasion of the forty-seventh birthday of the eminent composer Leonard Bernstein, his friend artist Larry Rivers drew a portrait of him. To testify to friendship for Bobby Short, the beloved cabaret singer who came to fame at the Carlyle singing the music of Gershwin and Cole Porter, painter Richard Merkin created a mural depicting Bobby among lines from the song "The Moving Picture Ball."

When his poet friends Wystan Auden, Edwin Muir, and St.-Jean Perse visited noted literary critic Edmund Wilson in his old family home in Talcottville, the weekend presents they left behind were fragments of verse engraved on the upstairs windows with a diamond pen. (Wilson always said that the diamond pen was the most inspired present his wife had ever given him.)

Not content with a verse, poet Rod McKuen wrote the whole marriage ceremony for his friend Jim Elliot's Malibu wedding, creating a true sixties happening that is not only still fondly remembered, but is immortalized in the plaster wedding cake slices that another good friend, Claes Oldenburg, ordered cast at a souvenir stand on the Santa Monica pier.

The ultimate gift between friends is the message of friendship. Cole Porter's "Easy to Love" was the song with which Jimmy Stewart surprised Carol Burnett at a Variety Club dinner at which she was the main honoree. (She had always looked up to him and had told him so.) Two years later, when asked to participate in the Kennedy Center tribute to Jimmy Stewart, "Easy to Love" was the song Carol Burnett chose to sing to her great and good friend.

RICHARD MERKIN
To
BOBBY SHORT

Above, Short and
"The Moving Picture Ball."

DWIGHT EISENHOWER
To
MILDRED HILSON

When President Eisenhower, better known for his military and political accomplishments than his painting, attempted a portrait of his friend New York philanthropist Mildred Hilson, he accompanied his work with a note of apology: "If you don't like the blob accompanying this note, file it in the garbage can."

In fact, Mrs. Hilson was thrilled. "The gift arrived in a brown paper package just before Christmas, marked: Eisenhower, Gettysburg, Pennsylvania. My heart went pitter-pat because I knew that whatever was in the package would be something I would always treasure. The package contained a framed portrait of me after a snapshot that the President had taken on a previous day. His taking the time to paint a portrait was beyond anything I ever expected."

Above, the snapshot from which Ike painted Hilson's portrait.

MOSHE DAYAN
To
BARBARA WALTERS

Barbara Walters' journalistic scruples are as famous as her skills, and as a result she has seldom become truly friendly with the celebrated figures she has interviewed. The notable exception was the late Moshe Dayan.

After granting her one of his rare interviews in the garden of his home in 1973, Dayan gifted Walters with a selection from his collection of archeological artifacts—a millennia-old bowl he had been using as an ashtray during their talk. Walters had admired it and, in an expansive gesture, he picked it up and inscribed it to her, leaving her little choice but to accept it.

There were other surprises in store. Having set the condition for the interview that his personal life was off limits, Dayan nevertheless proceeded to take her inside his home and introduced her to his wife. Seeing the bowl (actually a mortar), Mrs. Dayan absented herself to find its accompanying pestle, which the couple insisted Walters also take.

The mortar and pestle were the first tokens of what would become a long friendship. Walters holds dear a number of small artifacts given her by the Dayans on the occasions when they visited New York.

Above, Barbara Walters and Moshe Dayan on Issues and Answers.

To Barbara with love -
Rachel & moshe Dayan.
Judea B.C. 1500

Gaza B.C. 1500

Henry McIlhenny, Philadelphia's urbane heir to the McIlhenny gas meter fortune, is reminiscent of the protagonist of a Henry James novel. He collects choice antiques, he takes the cure in Montecatini, he dips into Salzburg for the music festival, and he stops by Venice when the crowds leave in September.

For many years he made his second home at Glenveagh in Ireland, a magnificent castle in what is known as the Scottish Baronial style, that was celebrated by the many friends who stayed there as an oasis of civilization and hospitality.

One of his regular guests was Loelia, Duchess of Westminster, who is known for her embroidery. One Christmas she made a drawing of the south side of the castle, including part of the lake and the garden. She then embroidered it and signed it with a strand of her own hair. To McIlhenny's amusement, she has asked him to will the piece to the National Trust, which plans a permanent exhibit of her handiwork.

Above, Glenveagh.

ANDY WARHOL
To
HENRY GELDZAHLER

Henry Geldzahler received as a birthday gift in the early 1970s a portrait done of him by artist and friend Andy Warhol. Geldzahler, former New York City cultural affairs chief, has strong ideas about what he likes; the portrait did not suit him at all, and he told Warhol so. "This is nothing but a Polaroid with a silk-screen added," he said. "You left out the art!"

A forgiving Warhol offered some years later to attempt another portrait. Geldzahler agreed, but asked him to be sure to put in the art this time. And this time, Geldzahler agrees, he did.

Mary Martin and several of her friends were gathered around her Christmas tree when the doorbell rang and a parcel in the shape of a book, wrapped in ordinary brown paper, with a letter attached, was delivered. Mary Martin didn't recognize the signature, but she soon realized that it was no ordinary book.

Page after page unfolded, each done in needlepoint, and each depicting a scene that was personal to her: a fragment of the last song that Oscar Hammerstein ever wrote for her, the ring that Richard Rodgers had given her, her signature motif of clasped hands—on and on through the events that Mary Martin had described in her autobiography as being the most meaningful in her life.

The letter, which was signed Susan Grushkin, recalled to her a correspondence they had had when Susan was a passionate eight-year-old fan. Those letters had encouraged Susan to go into dance. She was now a ballerina and, all these years later, had taken the time out from her life to extend to her idol her admiration and thanks. To Mary, this was truly "a labor of love."

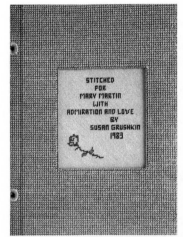 

Above, needlepoint pages from Mary Martin's album.

When Irene Selznick was looking for investors for her production of *A Streetcar Named Desire,* she turned confidently to her friend Jock Whitney, one of Broadway's better-known angels. Unbelievably, he turned her down. Irene was devastated. She pleaded that such an eminent refusal would doom the whole project. Somewhat reluctantly, Whitney relented and took one unit, but in his wife Betsey's name.

Streetcar's smash success is a matter of record, but Jock Whitney's reaction deserves more of an airing. Irene Selznick was preparing a party to mark the first anniversary of her hit.

She was wrapping gifts to give each cast member when the doorbell rang and in walked two men carrying a large shape. It was a streetcar and it was named *Desire,* and it had finely wrought details—pegged floors, tooled seat covers, and movable windows—that were obscured for the moment by an enormous confluence of ribbons that trailed across the floor and out to the elevator. The streetcar was Jock Whitney's acknowledgment that having his arm twisted hadn't been so painful after all. "And while I was busy thinking of everyone else," says Irene, "someone was thinking of me."

Above, Selznick's production of A Streetcar Named Desire.

GARY COOPER
To PABLO PICASSO

In 1957 Gary and Veronica "Rocky" Cooper were summering in the South of France when photographer David Douglas Duncan arranged for them to meet Pablo Picasso at La Californie. Cooper and Picasso got along famously and looked forward to meeting again the following summer.

After he met Picasso, Coop said "You're a hell of a guy, but I really don't get those pictures." "That doesn't matter," Picasso said. "If you really want to do something for me, get me one of those hats you wear in the movies."

Recalling a large table in Picasso's villa that was piled high with hats, Cooper resolved to top them all with an eagle-feather war bonnet.

Picasso was delighted with his gift and wore it often. "Voilà Geronimo!" he would exclaim, looking his fiercest, as in this moment captured so vividly by Duncan.

Above, the Coopers and the Picassos.

PAT BUCKLEY
To
BILL BLASS

Pat Buckley wanted to give Bill Blass a special birthday present, and she thought a firescreen painted with a portrait of Kate and Brutus, Blass's cherished golden retrievers, would be perfect. She assembled some snapshots of the dogs, cut wood to use as a ground—then realized that she was unsure of Katie's markings. Not a problem, she decided; she would simply telephone Blass's housekeeper.

"Mrs. Buckley, how would *I* know Katie's markings?" exclaimed the housekeeper. "And Katie has just rolled in a pile of cow dung!"

"Well, wash her off and call me back," was Mrs. Buckley's response.

The more formal portrait of Kate and Brutus, hanging on the wall, was also a birthday gift to Blass, this one painted by his friend New York socialite Annette Reed.

Above, Kate and Brutus.

164

BILL BLASS
To
PAT BUCKLEY

The friendship between noted fashion designer Bill Blass and Mrs. William F. Buckley extends beyond fashion to a shared passion for gardening and dogs, and this has provided the theme for the presents they exchange.

"For Christmas 1982, a drawing came for me from Bill and I looked at it, and I thought, how lovely, the first shoot of spring.

"And then, five minutes later—you know how at Christmas you open packages and glance to see what's inside without really taking in the contents—I put on my glasses; it was then that I realized Bill had drawn it, and it was really marvelous, just one solitary green shoot coming up out of the earth. I put it on a mother-of-pearl easel on a table in our country house. It is the first thing I see every morning."

Above, Bill Blass and Pat Buckley.

Leonard Bernstein To Aaron Copland

The whole world recognizes the distinctly American sound of Aaron Copland's music. His ballets such as *Rodeo* and *Appalachian Spring* and patriotic pieces such as the ever-popular *Fanfare for the Common Man* have defined an American orchestral tradition.

No man of music is more indebted to that tradition than Leonard Bernstein, another American musical original. Bernstein developed an early admiration for the older composer, whose success helped pave the way for his own achievements. Copland's early memories of Bernstein stem from having heard about a young student at Harvard "who plays your piano variations in a way that you ought to hear." Copland says, "When I heard those variations, my eyes opened wide. He was a very gifted guy."

For Copland's seventieth birthday, in 1970, Bernstein composed *Lenny B's Canon in Aaron's Mood*. Copland cherished it along with the outpourings of good wishes he received from musical notables all over the world.

Above, Aaron Copland and Leonard Bernstein.

Jimmy Stewart was devoted to a quarter horse called Pie, that he rode for twenty-one years in nineteen Westerns. He was so fond of Pie that when he came to Santa Fe in 1969 to make *The Cheyenne Social Club* with Henry Fonda, he sent for his favorite. "I had been watching Pie and he was showing his age and you could see him starting to get a swayback. But I wanted to see him, so he was trucked to Santa Fe. The trouble is Santa Fe is almost 7,000 feet above sea level, which made it tough, and after a couple of tries I knew the horse could not be used. So Pie stayed in the corral.

"Three days after we finished the film—it happened to be my birthday—Fonda came down with a package, and it was this painting of Pie, all framed and everything. He had done this for me, and it's been here ever since. We knew each other for over fifty years. We were very close friends, and this is a wonderful remembrance of him. He was very talented. The touching thing is that only ten days after Hank gave me the painting, Pie died."

Above, Henry Fonda and Jimmy Stewart in The Cheyenne Social Club.

Below, Grandma Moses and Lillian Gish.

GRANDMA MOSES
To
LILLIAN GISH

Lillian Gish: "Grandma Moses gave me this painting a little after I did the film *Grandma Moses*. She came to my home for dinner with her daughter. Her daughter was an old woman, but Grandma wasn't. She didn't know how to say no, and she didn't know about the market value of her paintings. Nancy Hamilton, writer and producer of such musical reviews as *One for the Money* and *Two for the Show*, wanted to buy one, but it was too expensive, and Grandma said, 'We could cut it in two and sell her half.'

"I remember asking her, 'Grandma, you have lived so much longer than I, are there things you know that you could tell me that would help me with my life?' And she thought for a long time and said, 'You know, if I have a problem, I do the very best I can; and then I say, *Ish kabibble*, which in real language means It's in God's hands.' It was so beautiful for her to tell me that. Grandma to me represented what America was all about."

SIR DANIEL J. DONAHUE
To
ANN AND RICHARD MILLER

No matter how busy her schedule as a leader of ARCS (Achievement Rewards for College Scientists) Foundation and as the mother of ten keeps her, San Franciscan Ann Miller sets aside time for her involvement with the Catholic Church. Ann and her husband, Richard, have a dear friend in Sir Daniel Donahue, who is a similarly active supporter of the church. So when Donahue gave his friends a tabernacle, or portable shrine, for their twenty-fifth wedding anniversary, it seemed an appropriate gift.

It was also a valuable one: "There are several in the Metropolitan Museum of Art," says Ann. But she will tell you that the true value of this gift lies in its meaning. "It is the sort of shrine that people used for private devotions or might have taken along when they traveled. Inside it, artistically represented, are the fifteen mysteries of the Catholic faith that correspond to the groups of beads on the rosary."

Above, Ann and Richard Miller.

171

ALFRED LUNT
To
HELEN HAYES

The great American actor Alfred Lunt, who enjoyed tracking things to their source, was tracing the steps of the legendary Sherlock Holmes to his Baker Street abode when he came across a curio shop that had an unusually fine collection of Victorian valentines. He had been looking for a present for Helen Hayes, America's first lady of the theater, who was in Chicago playing *Victoria Regina*. What could be more appropriate than a Victorian valentine? Ten Victorian valentines, decided Lunt, and promptly bought them all.

Forty years later, they remain among Miss Hayes' dearest treasures. "They are the most rich and exquisite I have ever seen. I had such a large collection of Victoriana by the end of the play's run that eventually I had to let it go. But the valentines I kept."

Another treasured gift from the same time is the miniature shadowbox given to Miss Hayes by Narcissa Thorne. It shows Queen Victoria in her drawing room.

Above, Helen Hayes as the young Victoria Regina.

Silk Stockings is noteworthy in the life of Cole Porter as the last of his Broadway shows and the only one to open after the death of his beloved wife, Linda. The cigarette case shown here, only one of scores he was given during his lifetime, is exceptional because it was *not* a gift from Linda but a gift given in her memory.

Throughout the thirty years of their marriage, Linda Lee Porter marked the opening of each of her husband's shows and movies with a specially designed cigarette case. All different and all wonderful, they found their way into Cole's pocket on opening night, talismans of his success. Though Linda was too ill to attend the May 7, 1953, debut of *Can-Can*, a Verdura case made its way there.

When *Silk Stockings* premiered, on February 24, 1955, Linda was gone—but not the tradition. Cole's good friends Jean Howard, Baron Nicholas de Gunzburg, Howard Sturges, Fulco di Verdura, and Mrs. John C. Wilson presented him with this Verdura cigarette case. Years later, it turned up for auction. Jean Howard was abroad at the time but enlisted a friend to submit the winning bid. "I just couldn't stand the idea that it would go to some stranger," she said.

Above, Cole Porter and Jean Howard.

Goodbye
& love
Cole

Roger de Garate To Byron Janis

Byron Janis, acclaimed concert pianist: "When I succeeded Roger de Garate as president of The Friends of Chopin in France, founded by him, he gave me various things in his possession. He greatly admired the way I played Chopin and particularly wanted me to have this death mask of the composer, which was made by George Sand's son-in-law, the French sculptor Auguste Clésinger.

"In those days, when someone died, it was very much in vogue to take an impression of the face in wax and then cast it in plaster. This mask of Chopin is one of the only two originals. It was in George Sand's house at Nohant, where she and Chopin lived together for some eight years and where the composer wrote so many of his greatest works.

"The strange thing is that twenty-five years before, I had visited Nohant, where I accidentally met and spent an entire day with Aurore, George Sand's granddaughter. This mask of Chopin had been given as a gift to Roger by Aurore. So you can imagine the extraordinary meaning this gift had for me."

Above, Byron Janis.

GERTRUDE LAWRENCE
To OSCAR HAMMERSTEIN II

In 1952, when Rodgers and Hammerstein's *The King and I* had been running for a year, cartoonist Steig did some charming caricatures for *Vogue* of the Siamese children in the production. Gertrude Lawrence, who was the first Mrs. Anna, loved them and felt that if they could be copied as figurines, they would make wonderful presents to those who had contributed so outstandingly to the musical's success.

She consulted New York jeweler Seaman Schepps, who rose to the occasion with these enchanting characters, which were carved out of ivory and painted by hand. The star to whom they owed so much bestowed on Yul Brynner, the King, and Dorothy Sarnoff, who played Lady Thiang, one of the figures and gave Hammerstein a full set.

Above, Gertrude Lawrence in The King and I.

Fleur Cowles
𝒯ₒ Jerome Zipkin

Real estate investor Jerome Zipkin has a collection of Meissen black-and-white leopards. Once, while in England, he asked artist Fleur Cowles to lunch. She was much taken with one of the porcelains and asked to borrow it for the weekend. It was returned in good order with a note of thanks. Some time later, in New York, he received in the mail this rendering of the leopard, with Fleur's signature rose in its mouth. It was her expression of gratitude for the inspiration it had given her to embark on her now celebrated series of animal paintings. The gift is a cherished part of Jerome Zipkin's art collection.

Jerome Robbins' dog, Nick, was a gift from his friends Lady Nancy Keith and Aiden Mooney. With this man's-best-friend, it was love at first sight: "I looked down at him and that was it, I knew I was stuck." Five years later, Robbins was distraught to find that the dog had disappeared.

"I went to the ASPCA, put ads in the paper, and even did interviews with NBC and CBS. Finally, I got a lead." Robbins was told that a neighborhood derelict had been seen with the dog, and he waited hours for the man on a street he was known to frequent. Derelict and

LADY NANCY KEITH
AND AIDEN MOONEY
To
JEROME ROBBINS

dog finally turned up, and Robbins went to get a policeman.

"By this time, they had entered a deserted building and the dog was barking at everybody and finally the policeman got him out. As soon as Nick saw me he jumped into my arms.

"I took Nick home and bathed him and he slept for five days. The following week, NBC did a follow-up story, and after that when I walked down the street with him, people would stop and say, 'That's the dog that was on television,' and in my neighborhood, where they had known me for years, they finally discovered who I was: 'You're that ballet guy who owns Nick, aren't you?' The dog was more famous than I was."

Above, Robbins and Nick.

DAVID HOCKNEY
To
BILLY AND AUDREY WILDER

Artist David Hockney: "It was an impulse. I had just finished a large painting that was based on a Ravel opera, with shepherds and shepherdesses and vivid colors. And I thought, We should light it and give a dinner right there in the studio, against the painting. And I thought, I'll give it for Billy Wilder. We've known each other a long time. I like him. We get along very well; he comes up regularly to see what I'm working on. He's seen everything I've ever done. And I'm a great admirer of his work, I think I've seen every film he's ever made.

"So it seemed like a good idea to give this dinner for Billy. I got someone to cater it

and we matched up the magenta and blue from the painting with the napkins and tablecloth. They asked if I wanted flowers. I said no, I'd do the flowers. So I made sculptures of flowers for everyone to take home, and then for the place cards I made a little painting of a shepherd or shepherdess with each guest's name.

"Twenty people came and we all sat at one long table: Billy and Audrey Wilder, Christopher Isherwood, Don Bachardy, Tony Richardson. All the people who had worked on the opera backdrop sat with their backs to the painting, and Billy and the others sat facing it so that they could enjoy the table against the painting."

Above, Billy Wilder.

183

TONY DUQUETTE
To
IRENE DUNNE

Artist Tony Duquette's imaginative works range from miniature fantasies of plumed headdresses and jeweled pendants to the dazzling City of the Angels, which he created for the bicentennial of Los Angeles.

More personal, though, was his gift to actress Irene Dunne, who starred in such films as *Love Affair, Theodora Goes Wild, The Awful Truth,* and *Life with Father,* of this elaborately encrusted Madonna holding a mandolin. Duquette has designed a number of Madonnas, but this one is particularly significant: not only is Dunne a devout Catholic, but hers is one of the few homes these days to possess a music room. Irene has great admiration for Tony as an artist and has spent many hours at his studio watching him work.

Above, Irene Dunne.

Barbara Hutton
To
Mary Lou Daves

As heiress to the Woolworth fortune, Barbara Hutton was spoiled and capricious. But she was as generous as she was demanding, tossing valuable presents to her friends: to Rosalind Russell when she was hospitalized, a gold-and-diamond bracelet hidden in a bouquet; to Elsa Maxwell when she admired it, a Fabergé cigarette case.

This purse, with its lapis-and-diamond clasp, is fashioned out of an antique altar cloth and was a surprise Christmas gift to Mary Lou Daves, the wife of Hollywood director Delmer Daves. Daves was then filming *Destination Tokyo,* which starred Barbara Hutton's husband of the moment, the dashing Cary Grant.

Above, Cary Grant and Barbara Hutton. Mary Lou Young and Delmer Daves.

PHYLLIS GEORGE
To
BOB EVANS

Wedding presents are an age-old custom, but how often does one hear of a divorce present? Among her many talents, anchorperson and former Miss America Phyllis George is an accomplished pianist. She had always wanted an early Steinway, and shortly after marrying Hollywood producer Bob Evans she found the piano of her dreams. The beautiful instrument was made in 1872, its glossy frame carved entirely of rosewood.

The piano was part of an estate, and so it was some time before it arrived in the Evans living room. The Evanses were thrilled to see that it fit into the room as if made for it.

The marriage lasted less than a year, but when the piano's ardent possessor started to pack up her treasure, she changed her mind. "It is too beautiful here," she said, "I can't take it from you; it is yours."

MERLE OBERON
To
EARL BLACKWELL

Chronicler of the celebrated, Earl Blackwell, editor of *The Celebrity Register*: "Merle Oberon and I were good friends from those days in the fifties when we would meet at various of Conrad Hilton's glamorous openings. When she married Rob Wolders, they would come to New York and stay with me.

"Merle knew I had acquired a collection of Chinese porcelain, so on one of their visits she gave me this beautiful Chinese dog."

Above, Merle Oberon and Earl Blackwell.

ROBERT J. WAGNER
To
LEONARD GOLDBERG

Television producer Leonard Goldberg and Robert Wagner have been friends for many years. As Leonard's wife, Wendy, recalls: "It was in the fall of 1983. R.J. was doing a picture in Lisbon, and he knew that Lennie had always been dying to go there, so he encouraged him to come over and join him. Lennie was really tempted; he thought Lisbon sounded so ex-  otic, but he couldn't get away. So he said, 'I tell you what, old sport, old buddy; you take a picture for me in a white dinner jacket, sort of like the Bogart days, and then I will have a little souvenir of it.'

"So for Christmas, that's what R.J. did. He gave Lennie this photograph of himself in a dinner jacket, signed 'Lisbon '83. Here's Looking at You Len.'"

Above, Robert Wagner and Leonard Goldberg.

WINSTON CHURCHILL
To
LEWIS DOUGLAS

It was at a farewell dinner given by Winston Churchill for America's retiring Ambassador to the Court of St. James, Lewis Douglas, that the Ambassador received his most cherished present. Some years earlier, the Prime Minister, who was a painter of some talent, had sent out Christmas cards made up from his painting of circus elephants; Douglas had so loved the card that he had asked his illustrious friend to sign one and then had it framed.

Toward the end of dinner, the host clapped his hands and two footmen appeared at the end of the dining room, where the curtains were drawn. The lights dimmed, Churchill clapped again, and the footmen pulled open the curtains. There, in the spotlight, was the original oil of *The Circus*, the very personal gift that Britain's leader had reserved as a farewell to his friend.

When does a gift certificate become a gift? When it is a painting done by a famous artist for a close friend.

Artist George Grosz greatly appreciated the patronage of art collector Bernard Reis, and wanted to give him a watercolor for Christmas in 1942. However, he did not want to make any assumptions about which of his paintings his friend would like. The answer to the dilemma was this painted gift certificate, which Reis could exchange for the painting of his choice.

No one seems to remember whether Reis cashed in the certificate or not; if he did, Grosz was kind enough to let him keep it anyway. It now hangs on the wall of the home of Reis's daughter, Barbara.

GEORGE GROSZ
To
BERNARD REIS

CHRISTIAN BÉRARD
To
DIANA VREELAND

Empress of fashion Diana Vreeland: "One of the things I adore is this portrait painted for me in 1967 by my best friend in Paris, Christian Bérard. One day he came to see me and said, 'Diane, today I do your painting.' He had no canvas, no brushes, not even paper, but he had these tubes of black and white paint. I was wearing the most glorious pearls and I had this hat on—it was really just a veil and a bow, my husband used to call the picture *A Weasel with Pearls.*

"We got the back of a box and Christian started to paint. He squeezed oil out of the tubes and applied it with his fingers. 'Ah, Diane,' he said, applying more paint, wiping his hands on his pants. I was so happy. Next morning I called but he had left for Paris. 'For Paris? You have got to be kidding—he has my painting!'

"So he had gone, and since he was a little drunk that day he might never have remembered that he ever painted me, that he was even here. But I was not going to write and bore him. Then one day my staff was lunching in the kitchen, and the doorbell rang, and they opened the door just a crack and in comes the piece of cardboard and a voice says, 'Pour Madame.' Someone handed them my portrait and left, and I just adore it. My darling Bébé."

Above, Bérard fashion sketch.

PAULETTE GODDARD
To
GEORGE AND PHYLLIS SEATON

Above right, Paulette Goddard.

Paulette Goddard, the enchanting heroine of *Modern Times*, was as generous to her colleagues as to her friends. One day she called Phyllis Seaton, her dialogue director and friend, to advise her of a gift she had in mind to commemorate their collaboration in *Kitty*.

Bent on choosing something special, Goddard had consulted her husband, Burgess Meredith, for inspiration. He suggested that she imagine the Seaton's house burning and try to figure out the one thing Phyllis and her husband, director George Seaton, would try to retrieve. The answer was simple, so Paulette was calling to tell the Seatons that she had commissioned a portrait of their five-year-old daughter, Mary, to be painted by Paul Clemens.

The friendship between screenwriter Mart Crowley and beautiful Lenny Dunne was shaped by allusions to their favorite films. Lenny's prize possession is this silk pillow, which Mart had monogrammed *R de W* for Rebecca de Winter and then singed—as if it had survived the fire in *Rebecca*. "The salesgirl couldn't believe it—why would someone spend so much on a pillow and then set it on fire?"

She also would have been bewildered by Lenny's inspiration for Mart, suggested by *Gone with the Wind*. She had an artist paint a Southern mansion on a white china box. On it she wrote, in antique script, *A Trifle from Tara*. She filled the box with "earth" made from chalk, smashed it, and wrapped it in another box covered with green velvet like Tara's curtains.

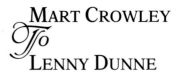

MART CROWLEY
To
LENNY DUNNE

WILLIAM BENTON
To
CLARE BOOTHE LUCE

Bill Benton was an achiever. At eighteen he went to Yale on a scholarship. At forty-three he became the publisher of the *Encyclopaedia Britannica,* and at forty-five he was made Assistant Secretary of State. Benton described himself as "a tactless and not too likable fellow, a shy man who conceals his shyness with a display of fervent purpose and alarming salesmanship"—qualities that did not immediately endear him to his classmate Henry Luce, the publisher of Time Inc., or to Luce's wife, Clare Boothe, when Benton looked them up in later years. In time, though, Benton's high ethical standards, his warmth, and his dedication to knowledge won them over.

Mrs. Luce treasures this jeweled elephant from Benton's Indian collection, given as a symbol of their friendship. It stands in front of Magritte's vision of her as a rose with a dagger, a reference to the diplomatic skill and the femininity of our former Ambassador to Italy—and to the flower that is her emblem.

Above, Clare Boothe Luce.

Albert Hadley, now a partner in the New York design firm Parish-Hadley, was a student at the Parsons School of Design when Van Day Truex was its director. Hadley would often stop by his office, which he recalls as a wonderful jumble of classical and modern: a very early Chinese lacquer table, an Eames chair, drawings by friends. In one corner stood this sculpture that Truex had brought from Paris, the first piece he had ever bought. (He had moved to Paris in the 1920s to direct the Parsons School there.) It was a working cast for a bust which had been commissioned by Queen Victoria. Hadley had always liked the bust, and it was always part of the scene, following Truex, who eventually became the chief designer of Tiffany, as he moved to various apartments.

Years later, in the late seventies, Hadley was dining at the home of Truex when he happened to open a closet and there on the floor was the bust. Hadley was delighted to see it again and asked why it was hidden away. "I have no place for it," replied Truex. "What a shame," said Hadley, "I love it so much." "Then you should have it," said Truex. Hadley accepted with alacrity and has enjoyed it ever since. "It has always represented Truex to me. The fascinating thing is the last time I saw Van, I dined with him one night and he had just bought a new bronze sculpture. A few weeks later he died. The executor of the will gave it to me. So I have the first and last pieces of sculpture that Van bought."

Above, Van Day Truex with sculpture.

COCO CHANEL
To
JOSHUA AND NEDDA LOGAN

Director Joshua Logan remembers: "In the late fifties, we were at a dinner party given by Mary-Louise Bousquet, who represented *Harper's Bazaar* and had one of the more amusing salons in Paris. Among the other guests was Coco Chanel, whom we had never met.

"As we passed into the dining room, our hostess turned to Chanel and said, 'You must meet the Logans, they have the most wonderful collection of mechanical dolls.' And Chanel exclaimed, 'Oh, how chic, I have only one, and it's theirs.'

"The next afternoon this wonderful automated blackamoor magician arrived at our hotel, St. James et d'Albany. I finally understood what that French expression 'Quel geste' meant. We had never met Chanel before and yet she gave us this outstanding piece for our collection."

THE GIFT OF

Largesse

Largesse is not learned; it is inborn, like laughter, like love. Uncontainable, irrepressible, and limitless, largesse is not a matter of fact but of degree, not how much you give but how much you give of what you possess. Like its affiliates, liberality and prodigality, largesse has *élan,* a talent for magnificence, a facility for excess.

The sanction of largesse is *carte blanche:* the order to spare no cost that Delmonico's received in succession from Messrs. Belmont, Travers, and Jerome, who had entered into competition as to who could give the ultimate dinner. Its manner is the grand gesture: Coco Chanel's superb riposte when she learned, upon meeting the Josh Logans, that they collected automata. "A collection. How chic! I have only one, and it is theirs."

The purveyors of largesse are the masters of grand giving. They may be imperious: "C'est mon plaisir" was the byword of Boston's Isabella Stewart Gardner, who once paid Paderewski three thousand dollars to play at tea time for herself and an elderly friend, on condition that he remain concealed behind a large screen. They may be misguided: when the Donohue boys were expelled from the Southampton Country Club, their mother, a Woolworth heiress, bought them the neighboring estate, upon which she had constructed the identical amenities. They may be presumptuous: Charles Revson would send lavish Christmas presents a day late so they would be remarked upon. Nevertheless, they retain a flair for the superlative and an inexhaustible determination to rid the world of dullness.

"He only is fit for this society who is magnanimous," said that true-bred New Englander Ralph Waldo Emerson, an indication that munificence is as American as apple pie. Its lineage, however, is considerably shorter. Our historical records stress the nation's frugality, and our social documents, like all literature, do best by the miser. Try to draw a face on Midas—but any schoolchild can conjure up the Scrooge-like figure of the first Rockefeller, rubbing his thin dimes. Stinginess makes better copy.

Furthermore, prodigality presupposes leisure and goods, and the frontiersman had little of either. Nor if he had, would he have known what to do with them. At a state dinner, when a waiter asked Abraham Lincoln, "Red or white?" the President said simply, "I don't know, which would *you?*"

One short generation later, America had a new royalty composed of railway barons, mining kings, merchant princes, and banking moguls, who carved out of sudden fortunes the art of being rich. These princes of privilege pioneered a formula for gilded living that would have dazzled the Sun King. Overnight they created a world as vivid as a hummingbird, if on a somewhat larger scale, in which a Fifth Avenue residence imitating the Château de Blois was the minimum collateral for social security. At the opera they perfected pomp, on their yachts they dallied with leisure, while at Newport and Palm Beach they invented conspicuous consumption. It was in this gilded era, as newly coined as the flashy word *millionaire,* that American munificence came of age.

It is important to remember that the American millionaire was truly that. Europe's wealthiest aristocrat was Archduke Frederick of Austria, whose estate before 1914 was valued at seven hundred fifty million dollars, and India's princes were said to be fabulously rich. But their wealth was frozen in land and jewels, whereas the Americans' assets could be instantly exchanged into goods or any world currency. No Europeans or Asians, in other words, approached in wealth the Rockefellers, Mellons, Fords, and du Ponts, whose fortunes individually could fund the Federal Reserve.

Money alone does not guarantee generosity. But if one leaves aside Hetty Green (who died worth one hundred million dollars, but whose son lost a leg because she was too mean to call a doctor) and J. Paul Getty (whose only present to his friend of many years Lady Diana Cooper was a used tube of balm for her arthritis), the vast fortunes of the American millionaires entailed a certain *largesse oblige.*

How could you be miserly if, like Nicholas Brady, your wealth bought the title of papal duke and a house whose dining room could serve fifteen hundred at one sitting? Why pinch pennies if you were Edward Berwind (who cozied his cottage in Newport with fifteen million dollars' worth of spoils from Venetian palaces), or Henry Ford II (who paid to reroute an offending highway because it passed too close to his property), or Joseph Pulitzer (who transported the entire New York Symphony Society orchestra to Bar Harbor to play for his guests)?

Why be stingy if, like Mrs. Dodge Sloane, you could import from France the pink soil for your tennis court; if, like best-dressed Mrs. Henry Clews of Newport, you could set aside ten thousand dollars annually for "mistakes in my clothes"; if, like Randolph Guggenheim, you could make headlines by hosting, at two hundred fifty dollars a plate, New York's costliest dinner, or, like Laura Gould, you could distribute Swiss real estate as party favors; if, like Charles Schwab, you could retain Caruso for ten thousand dollars to sing for your dinner guests; if, like Charles Munn, you could charter a Pan American jet to fly you directly to Palm Beach from Paris, in order to bypass the unpleasantness of JFK Airport; if, like William Leeds, you could lodge a hundred Lincolns in your garage; or if, like Thomas Fortune Ryan, you could buy the neighboring Fifth Avenue mansion expressly to demolish it to make room for a rose garden?

Even when taxes—and censure—toned down flamboyance and the Depression curtailed high-profile spending, it was hard to keep a grand man down. (When traction king Charles Yerkes was advised to tone down the bronze doors of his Fifth Avenue mansion in keeping with the new propriety, he obliged by coating them in platinum.) The great giver has come down to our time as an American archetype, the soft touch, the abundant person, who is born to the assumption that money grows on trees and who matures into the conviction that money, in the felicitous phrase of big spender Gene Fowler, "is to be thrown from moving trains."

Legend has it that one day as Samuel Newhouse was going to the newsstand for the paper, he asked his wife if there was something he could bring her. Yes, replied Mitzi, she would like *Vogue*. And he bought her Condé Nast. The story is apocryphal but symptomatic. The great giver operates in superlatives, helplessly expansive, hopelessly extravagant, never having learned the mathematics of doing things by halves.

When Broadway producer Harry Richman was enjoying the favors of Hollywood's "It" girl, Clara Bow, he would send her flowers each time they made love (the florist bill for one week listed thirty dozen gardenias and a dozen orchids), and he overwhelmed her with truckloads of very large presents—a bearskin rug, a Great Dane, building up to the crescendo of a Steinway baby grand. "But I don't play the piano," she protested. Never mind; it was big. When impresario Flo Ziegfeld made his first bid for the attention of soubrette Anna Held, he delivered backstage a basket of rare orchids concealing a diamond bracelet. The following night Anna received a second arrangement just like the first. "But," she demurred, "you gave me a diamond

Below, Clara Bow and Harry Richman.

Above, Florenz Ziegfeld and Anna Held.

bracelet yesterday." Never mind; he had sparked her interest.

The great giver must have a sense of occasion. Judging "I do" too prosaic for his wedding vows to Isobel McCreery, San Francisco's Augustus Taylor hired an airplane to banner the garden party with a smoky "I love you." When young Charlie MacArthur first met Helen Hayes at a cocktail party, all he could think to offer her was a bagful of peanuts. "I wish they were emeralds," he said with a smile—which won him her heart and her hand. Years after, when he returned from service in India, he held out to her another brown bag, saying, as the emeralds spilled out on her lap, "I wish they were peanuts."

The great giver acts on impulse. One summer day Ernest Dane of Boston was visiting Hill, the noted English violin maker, when the great cellist Gregor Piatigorsky, then still very young, stopped in for a repair on his serviceable but unremarkable cello. While waiting, Piatigorsky began playing on a fine Montagnana in the showroom. Dane listened attentively, then spoke to Hill and took his leave. When the young cellist finished playing, Hill said to him, "I have just been advised that the Montagnana is yours."

The grand gesture stands apart, the province of those who, as Stanley Marcus once put it, "if they don't know precisely what, know they want something big or frequent or special or outstanding or forever." He was referring to the likes of *bon vivant* Dick Andrade, who asked Marcus to advise him on a Christmas present for his wife. "Let's look at the store windows," suggested the prince of merchants, leading him to Neiman's lavish display of choice items. "I'll take that one," said Andrade. "That bracelet?" asked Marcus. "No, that window." And down to the last glittering item, the entire display was set up behind cellophane and placed by the Andrades' tree to await Christmas morning. Marcus had in mind too the customer who came in one day and searched vainly through the emporium's twenty-five-million-dollar inventory for something special enough for his wife, until Marcus suggested layering pastel cashmere cardigans inside an over-size Steuben brandy glass, topping them with a white angora pullover and, for the cherry, a ruby ring. "A parfait!" exclaimed the seeker of the gift that says it all, "just what I was looking for!"

The maestro of éclat would have approved of Beverly Hills jeweler Francis Klein's prominent client, who stopped in with his wife to buy her a little something. Several large purchases later, he was steering her toward the door when she saw a necklace in the window she absolutely had to have, a magnificent antique piece set with scarabs and gold. "Enough is enough," said her visibly irritated husband, who had yet to pack for their return flight to New York. The next morning the Kleins were awakened by a phone call. Would they both be so obliging as to bring the necklace to New York? A suite had been reserved for them at the Pierre and a table was booked the following evening at Romeo Salta. Would they be there and go along with the charade of, "What a coincidence! You *must* join us for dinner," and then, during cocktails, slip him the necklace? Not ones to spoil the fun, the Kleins complied, and they were rewarded by an expression they call indescribable as there emerged from the martini of their client's unsuspecting wife not an olive, but six gleaming scarabs.

The great giver's credentials are flair and panache. Ryan O'Neal qualified when he brought Joe Cocker along to sing "Happy Birthday" to a friend. Sammy Davis Jr. became eligible when for his wife Altovise's birthday he presented her with a first-class round-trip ticket to Paris, a suite for two weeks at the George V, and a blank check for a shopping spree. Producer Jerry Weintraub made it when the columnist Joyce Haber, having apologized for the appearance of her car when she arrived to interview him, returned home to find his chauffeur waiting to wash and polish it.

Jewelry designer Kenneth Jay Lane joined the club when he insisted that dancer Maya Plisetskaya keep the armful of bracelets she was admiring in his showroom, asking only that she perform on the spot her rendition of the dying swan in *Swan Lake*.

Producer Richard Cohen entered the lists when, after a red-and-white-striped Turnbull & Asser shirt he wore to a luncheon was much admired by colleague Leonard Goldberg, he invited the same group to dinner several weeks later and donned the same shirt. "That great shirt again," Goldberg noted. "For you, Lennie, the shirt off my back," said Cohen—and to the delight of his guests, he proceeded to strip. However, modesty was preserved; under the shirt was its duplicate, ordered from London in the interim.

Leba Sedaka joined the ranks when she offered her husband a Bentley in a jewelry box. A week before, singer Neil Sedaka had seen a Bentley he was crazy about but reasoned himself out of. He then changed his mind, but when he contacted the seller, the car had been sold. The jewelry box that

Jean Flagler Matthews
To
Joseph Serzan

Above, the Miss Flagler.

Leba carefully placed on his birthday plate was powerless to lift his spirits—until he discovered that it held the key to his dream car.

Paul Newman earned membership when he flew his wife, Joanne Woodward, to a remote beach in Hawaii for dinner *à deux*. It had been done before, of course, but Newman went the extra distance, providing a new evening dress for the occasion and a quartet to serenade them as they dined together in style.

Style is the shape and the form of largesse. When the biggest chips are down, when all the aces are on the table, it is not expenditure but style that marks the unforgettable gesture. Mrs. Jean Flagler Matthews, devoted to the captain who had served the Flagler family for over forty years, had always promised him burial at sea. Little did he suspect that when the final moment came, she would have him towed into the Atlantic on her very own yacht, and that there, in the crisp morning of a perfect day at sea, captain and ship would be scuttled together.

Style is not the content but the manner of giving. "I enjoy making the proper presentation," Walter Annenberg once said, "Presentation is almost everything." It was everything for Buster Keaton, the silent-screen comedian, who undertook to play out a cherished fantasy with his young wife. He ordered construction of a villa in the Hollywood Hills in complete secrecy. "It had to be all done, with every stick of furniture in place, before I'd casually drive by with Natalie and she'd say, 'What a dear house' and I'd say, 'It's yours.'"

By the time singer Kenny Rogers was inspired to do something similar for wife Marianne, Hollywood had become such a fishbowl that, to prevent her from hearing about the Malibu beach house he had chosen for her Christmas present, Rogers took her to Europe while the work was being done. On their return, he had the entire house decorated in holly and pine, then took her by "to drop in on a friend." Only when Marianne read the plaque on the door, Casa de Marianna, did she guess. "My hands got tingly and tears came to my eyes. I could not believe it was actually mine."

More elaborate still was the much earlier gesture of Samuel Gessford, a contractor of Washington, D.C. To stave off his young wife's homesickness for her native Philadelphia, he took her to Europe while he erected, across from their Capitol Hill home, five row houses in the style of those in her home town. They returned to Washington late in

Samuel Gessford
To His Wife

Above, Philadelphia Row in Washington, D.C.

the night, and when she looked out her window the next morning, she saw Philadelphia.

Posterity has not recorded whether the great opera singer Ganna Walska was equally enchanted when she awoke on her birthday to find her lawn carpeted in machinery: her suitor, Chicago magnate Harold McCormick, had dispatched to her chateau in Versailles one of every type of harvester his company produced. But Margo Albert clearly recalls every moment of the dawn when her husband, actor Eddie Albert, orchestrated spring. They had just moved into a new house, very large, very pretty, but with no flowers at all. It was the cusp of the new season; "I needed so much to see flowers. We had planted a few things, but nothing had come up. Then one morning very early, the time both of us love, Eddie said, 'Come, there is something popping out of the ground.' And I went to the balcony and there were hundreds and hundreds of daffodils in full bloom, standing tall and golden yellow in the dawn's early light."

Equally well remembered was the delight of Texas oil millionaire Jake Hamon, who returned with his wife, Nancy, to their suite at the Ritz in Paris after a matinee of *Love in the Afternoon* to find it converted into the film's most famous scene. There was the veiled lady, the violinists, and, among the genuine guests waiting to sing "Happy Birthday," Maurice Chevalier himself. Chevalier would later pronounce Nancy Hamon's *tour de force* "d'une générosité et encore." It was generous and it was something more.

Style is what propels generosity into largesse, catapults the memorable into the immortal. Generosity is the fresh flowers that producer David O. Selznick had delivered every day to actress Jennifer Jones after they were married. Style is the bouquet of red roses that baseball great Joe DiMaggio sent every week to be placed on the grave of Marilyn Monroe, his one-time wife, for twenty years following her death.

Generosity is the gesture of Ewing Kauffman, who purchased the Kansas City Royals baseball team "because my wife wanted them." Style is the resolution of David Stickelber of Kansas City to place Oriental rugs in the kitchen "because it keeps the help happy." Generosity is buying out Bloomingdale's for your wife, as Charles Revson liked to do. ("It was a pleasure to go shopping with him," recalls his wife. "Anything that looked good on you, you could have.") Style is arranging for Bloomingdale's to stay open after hours, as producer Lou

Below, the Albert family.

Below, Jennifer Jones and David O. Selznick.

Above, Hamon with Maurice Chevalier at Love in the Afternoon *party.*

Above, Rosalind Russell and husband Frederick Brisson.

PRISCILLA PRESLEY
To
ELVIS PRESLEY

Above, Presley's gold piano.

Adler did, so that his girlfriend could shop there undisturbed.

Generosity is the piano Priscilla Presley had gilded to present to her flash-loving husband, Elvis Presley. Style is the concert grand piano Yoko Ono and John Lennon gave to their friend Sam Green. Delivery had to be on Thanksgiving, the day they preferred to Christmas for gift giving, and a complete surprise. Notwithstanding the red tape and the traffic arising from Macy's Thanksgiving Day parade, while Green was hauled off to feast with cooperative friends, the Lennons had the entire block between Fifth and Madison closed off, moved in a crane, and hauled the massive instrument through the French windows of the ballroom. Presumably, a tuner was similarly hoisted, because Green returned from his turkey and mince to find the piano not only artfully placed but perfectly tuned.

Generosity is the almost reckless abandon with which Barbara Hutton gave jewelry to her friends. Style is her get-well gesture to Rosalind Russell, a gold-and-diamond bracelet embedded in roses. "I couldn't possibly accept it," protested her friend. "But you must," countered Barbara. "I specially chose it to go with your wedding ring." High style is her sensitivity to Signora Cabatta, the nurse who had seen her through an illness in Rome and whom she had rewarded with a bracelet from Bulgari. Cabatta was overwhelmed but embarrassed: "I am a simple woman," she ventured and asked if she might trade the precious piece for a kidney operation her husband needed. Barbara's check was made out forthwith.

Style is getting it right—not always easy. When a woman from the Tennessee mountains wrote to Grace Kelly, asking for something nice to wear to her children's school meetings, the actress sent an item from her wardrobe far more difficult for her to part with than a ball gown, but the only one she judged suitable, a favorite, quite ordinary but very serviceable, green corduroy suit. It was returned at once, with no explanation. Grace Kelly had completely missed the point: her petitioner craved glamour, not utility.

Style is refusing to call in the chips. Raymond Loewy, the industrial designer noted for the Studebaker and the Lucky Strike logo, once pointed out to President Kennedy that the appointments of *Air Force One* left much to be desired. He was immediately commissioned to overhaul the aircraft, which he did, waiving his fee. Nor would he accept remuneration for the commemorative stamp that Jackie requested he design after the assassination.

Lincoln Kirstein asked composer Igor Stravinsky, in his capacity as "father and future" of the New York City Ballet, to compose a fanfare for the 1964 opening of Philip Johnson's New York State Theater. Kirstein meant the work to be a gift for their friend and colleague George Balanchine. Stravinsky deplored that pressing work on *Variations*, which he had already interrupted to compose *Elegy for J.F.K.*, would preclude such a commitment, but two days later he composed *Fanfare for a New Theater* and dedicated it as a gift "To Lincoln and George."

Generosity assigns the grand giver a place in our hearts; style places him in the pantheon of the immortals. J.P. Morgan kept a tailor in residence at his hunting lodge in Scotland so that he could bestow a complete shooting outfit upon each of his guests. When William Randolph Hearst's chauffeur ran over a goose on a back road in France, Hearst promptly fired the chauffeur and sent the farmer, by way of apology, a live goose encased in a new Renault.

Another immortal was James Gordon Bennett, mogul of the *Herald*. When he failed to find a table at his favorite eatery in Monte Carlo, Bennett bought the establishment on the spot. He dined to his satisfaction on their inimitable lambchops, and then gave the restaurant as a tip to the waiter who served him. Exceptional too was Marjorie Merriweather Post, who in her absence arranged for a few days of luxury for her children's tutor, lodging him in the master suite, putting her car and chauffeur at his disposal, and leaving for his pleasure a pile of invitations to the key debutante balls.

If one were to draw up a coat of arms for the mightiest givers of them all, the heraldic devices might be a pair of garters, a house in Bel Air, and a lark. The garters would be Noel Coward's. One evening in Paris, as Moss Hart recounts it, he and Coward met for cocktails at the Ritz. Some time between the first *kir* and the third, Hart presented his old friend with a pair of gold garters. Coward donned them immediately, bequeathing his old ones with a flourish to the bartender—but not before Hart noticed that they too were made of gold.

The house would be one that millionaire engineer Lynn Atkinson intended as a surprise for his wife. He bought twelve acres at 750 Bel Air Road and hired architect Sumner Spalding to build a forty-room mansion of such grandeur and costliness that it took three years to complete. When all was ready, Atkinson orchestrated a radiant party—flowers, musicians, friends—and all waited to surprise Mrs. Atkinson, who had been told only to dress formally because business acquaintances were giving a dinner. As they drove up the elaborate driveway, she remarked disapprovingly to her husband, "Who could possibly live in such a pretentious place?" "Let's go then," he replied. "This is one party we don't have to stay at." He drove away; they never moved into the house.

The lark would be the bird that Charles Lang Freer, the noted art collector and patron of Whistler, promised to send back to Whistler's wife from his forthcoming sojourn in India. He ventured deep into the interior, contracting jungle fever, but finally located a pair of the rare singing birds. One survived the trip back, bringing Beatrice Whistler great joy. Two years later she died, and Whistler wrote to Freer: "She loved the wonderful bird you sent with such happy care from the distant land! And when she went—alone because I was unfit to go too—the strange wild dancing creature stood uplifted on the topmost perch and sang and sang as it had never sung before! A song of the sun—and of joy—and of my despair! Loud and ringing clear from the skies!—And louder! Peal after peal—until it became a marvel the tiny breast, torn by such glorious voice, should live! And suddenly, it was made known to me that in this mysterious magpie waif from beyond the temples of India, the spirit of my beautiful Lady had lingered on its way—and the song was *her* song . . . and so was her farewell."

In the ultimate gesture, the gift and the giver and the recipient become one.

CONCLUSION

*K*nowing that his wife was as passionate about gardening as she was devoted to good works, William Astor once gave her the choice: "Should I give you money to establish an orphanage, Peachy, or to build a greenhouse?" Margaret replied at once: "I would dearly love to have a greenhouse, but as I am a good Christian woman I know that an orphanage should come first." "That is the right answer," said her husband. "You shall have both." Both Margaret's response and William's were characteristic of a national temperament endowed with what F. Scott Fitzgerald described as "willingness of heart."

Unpredictably, from beginnings that were almost dismally frugal, Americans developed a structure of giving unparalleled in the Western world. Andrew Carnegie, the steel king, could have been America's first billionaire. Instead he gave away in the space of eighteen years 90 percent of his fortune, and when his secretary warned him he was dipping into capital, his gleeful reply was, "Delighted to hear it, my boy, keep it up." John D. Rockefeller, of the parsimonious reputation, gave away $750 million in his lifetime; his son, John D., Jr., gave away $457 million. Vincent Astor, with foresight and determination, drove the remainder of his family's great fortune into the terminal of the Astor Foundation.

There were more personal gestures. William H. Vanderbilt brought Cleopatra's Needle from Egypt as a gift to Central Park. Coal magnate Samuel In-sull gave Chicago its Opera House. The great financier Otto Kahn divested himself of two million dollars to restore the ailing Metropolitan Opera to New York. Henry Clay Frick conceived his Fifth Avenue mansion from its inception as a museum to be given to the city. Andrew Mellon, who at the time of his appointment as Secretary of the Treasury was listed in *The New York Times* as "an unknown millionaire from Pittsburgh," gifted Washington with the National Gallery, which, together with such bequests as Raphael's *Alba Madonna,* Botticelli's *Adoration of the Magi,* and Van Eyck's *Annunciation,* totaled a gift to the nation of a staggering fifty million dollars.

The advent of the income tax in 1913 and the inheritance tax in 1935 may have modified the altruism of the giving incentive. But to dismiss out of hand their instinct for giving would be to do a grave injustice to our nation's great benefactors. For them, beneficence was important, their chief motive for spending, their prime means of expression.

The instinct for giving motivated virtually all the Guggenheims. When Simon married Olga Hirsh in 1898, he underwrote a turkey dinner for a thousand of Denver's impoverished youths. When Daniel heard about the San Francisco fire of 1906, he cabled fifty thousand dollars with the instruction: NO RED TAPE GIVE IT TO THE PEOPLE AT ONCE. When Eleanor received fifty thousand dollars on her engagement to Viscount Stuart, she divided it among her favorite charities. Murry provided free dental service for the poor of New York, and Solomon gave the city its uptown modern museum, encased in a Frank Lloyd Wright masterpiece.

Giving was instinctive to the irrepressible Alma Spreckels, wife of the sugar king, whose gift of Rodin's *Thinker* to the City of San Francisco represented some sacrifice, since she had to pawn several pieces of jewelry to raise the fourteen thousand dollars the casting was commanding.

So immersed in the spirit of giving was Abby Aldrich Rockefeller, the wife of John D., Jr., that one Christmas during World War II she sent a present to every soldier in her son's regiment. He tried to dissuade her, but she persisted in mailing nine thousand gifts: "I don't want a single man not to have some remembrance."

Such was the impulse to give of the Leland Stanfords that upon the death of their promising only child, they endowed Stanford University with twenty-eight million dollars, willing that "The children of California shall be our children."

The expansive boundaries of American benevolence serve to confirm that we are a nation of givers. Just as on the public front we have moved outward from the dozen dishcloths that the first John Jacob Astor dropped off at an orphanage to the vast reaches of philanthropy, so have we in our private lives moved inward from the elaborate gift prescribed for a conventional occasion to the meaningful present that, regardless of its value, we hold absolutely without price, given as it is for reasons of sentiment, because it is Monday, or the first day of spring.

We have learned to exchange fabulous presents—yachts and mansions and diamonds in imperial settings. We have also learned the value of a single blossom and a verse etched on a windowpane.

We have learned to give gifts for a reason and for no reason at all; gifts to say thank you, get well, welcome home, and we love you; gifts from the pocketbook and gifts from the heart.

We have come to understand that true giving takes place in a realm above fad and above fashion, where wealth becomes synonymous with grace and the only diamonds that are a girl's best friend are diamonds set in love. Trends may change, but presents will never become a minority taste, because in a world of shifting values generosity remains an absolute.

At its finest, the true gift is incandescent, as was the gesture of prince of public relations Robert Gray, who, to mark the birthday of his dear friend Mildred Hilson, had the Eiffel Tower illuminated for five minutes. It is the token or treasure that lights up the other person, that clarifies a friendship, that remains a luminous memory long after the gift itself may have dematerialized.

At its purest, the true gift is itself a form of love, of perfected communication, in which everything that is meaningful between two people is expressed through what is given and received. The true gift, when the gift and the feeling are one, is the most tangible sign of human devotion, the salient symbol of the willing heart.

INDEX OF NAMES

PHOTOGRAPH CREDITS

The publishers acknowledge with thanks the following sources of auxiliary photographs:

Claude Azoulay, 188; The Bettmann Archive, 14, 20 (bottom left and right), 161, 205; Edward Marshall Boehm, Inc., 93; Dan Brinzac, 51; Wendy Cooper, 40; David Douglas Duncan, 162, 163; Johnny Engstead, 94; Mary Anne Fackelman, 26; The Fine Arts Museums of California, 124, 125; Ray Fisher, 115; The Henry Morrison Flagler Museum, 14, 207; FORBES Magazine Collection, 103; Toni Frissell, 58; Galerie St. Etienne, 170 (right); Jonathan M. Gibson, 155; Globe Photos, 209 (top right); Philippe Halsman, 199; Mark Ivins, 166; Jim Johnson, 32; The John Fitzgerald Kennedy Library, 73; Jay Kupjack, 53, 77 (right); Christopher Little, 108; Movie Star News, 31, 87, 169, 185, 196 (right), 205 (top left and right); Museum of the City of New York, 19, 147; Hans Namuth, 131; David Payne, 43; Wilbur Pippin, 201; The Preservation Society of Newport County, 35; Matthew Ralston, 25; Robert Reck, 119; Rodgers & Hammerstein Theatre Library, 106; Mark Segal, 81, 106 (top right), 195 (right); Smithsonian Institution, 94 (top left); Sotheby's, 20 (top right); Le Studio Peguy, 94; Curtice Taylor, 49; Thomas P. Vinetz, 94 (bottom right); White House Collection, 92; Will Rogers Museum, 141; The Woodrow Wilson House Museum, The National Trust for Historic Preservation, 91; Walter Zeboski, A.P., 42.